THE ATLANTIC CRITICAL STUDIES

WILLIAM SHAKESPEARE'S
Othello

THE ATLANTIC CRITICAL STUDIES

WILLIAM SHAKESPEARE'S *Othello*

RATRI RAY

ATLANTIC
PUBLISHERS & DISTRIBUTORS (P) LTD

Published by

ATLANTIC

PUBLISHERS & DISTRIBUTORS (P) LTD

7/22, Ansari Road, Darya Ganj,
New Delhi-110002
Phones : +91-11-23273880, 23275880, 23280451
Fax : +91-11-23285873
Web : www.atlanticbooks.com
E-mail : info@atlanticbooks.com

Branch Office
5, Nallathambi Street, Wallajah Road,
Chennai-600002
Phones : +91-44-64611085, 32413319
E-mail : chennai@atlanticbooks.com

Printed in India at Nice Printing Press, A-33/3A, Site-IV, Industrial Area, Sahibabad, Ghaziabad, U.P.

General Preface

The Atlantic Critical Studies, are study-aids modeled on the study-aids available in England and America, among other places, and are primarily meant for the students of English the literature of Indian universities.

However, in consideration of the local conditions and the various constraints under which our students have to study—the models our students have to study—non-availability of relevant critical books, dearth of foreign and Indian journalism inaccessibility to good, well-equipped libraries, just to mention a few of them—the models have been considerably improved upon both qualitatively and quantitatively.

Thus while these studies are meant to be comprehensive and self-sufficient, the distinguished scholars who have prepared these study materials, have taken special care to combine lucidity and profundity in their treatment of the texts.

The Select Bibliography at the end is meant not only to acknowledge the sources used but also to help a student in the pursuit of further studies if s/he wants to.

Atlantic believes in quality and excellence. These studies will only reconfirm it.

Mohit K. Ray
Chief Editor [English Literature]
Atlantic Publishers & Distributors,
New Delhi

Contents

1

Introduction

It has been observed by E.M.W. Tillyard that whereas the spirit of the Renaissance had expressed itself through painting in Italy, in England it did so through literature. The Elizabethan Age is the best, the Golden Age of England and it expresses the Renaissance spirit to perfection. Shakespeare is the best product of it.

One of the special features of the Elizabethan genius is its versatility, and Shakespeare possessed it in full measure. He tried his hand at all kinds of plays, whether tragedy, or comedy, or chronicles, or romances. This cannot be said about every dramatist of his time. Marlowe and Ben Jonson wrote tragedies and satirical comedies respectively. Again, within the different categories of tragedy and comedy, there is more variety in Shakespeare than in anyone else. His tragedies range at will over space and time, covering different countries at different times. If the question of genre comes, all the four main kinds of tragedies current in Elizabethan times can be found among his works. There is Conqueror tragedy in *Macbeth*, Revenge tragedy in *Hamlet*, the Domestic tragedy in *Romeo and Juliet*. The play under discussion, *Othello* is a combination of the Domestic tragedy and the Villain tragedy. Moreover, such tags, though convenient, fail to convey the impression of richness and complexity that his plays give. A like variety is to be seen in the field of comedy as well, for he wrote Romantic comedies (*As You Like It*, etc.), Problem comedies (*Measure for Measure*), Fairy tales (*A Midsummer Nigtht's Dream*) and Romances as in the last play. As far as history plays are concerned, he wrote plays based on English as well as roman history. In each case, he took up a popular mode of the time and developed it to such an extent that it became a universal play while bearing the stamp of his genius.

He took the material for his play from many sources, like narrative poems, prose romances, old play, history books, etc. In each case, he took the available material and re-formed it, rejecting some details, concentrating some, expanding others, till the entire play became fully stage worthy and an immortal work of art.

The Elizabethan tragedy of blood and thunder has been divided into the four categories mentioned above; Conqueror tragedy, Revenge tragedy, Villain tragedy and Domestic tragedy. Shakespeare's tragedies can fall within them, but they soar beyond their many limitations. *King Lear*, for example, can hardly be contained within any one of them, and *Hamlet* is far more than a mere revenge tragedy. But besides this, there is another way of grouping his tragedies.

The Early Tragedies: *Titus Andronius, Romeo and Juliet.*
The Great Tragedies: *Hamlet, Othello, King Lear, Macbeth.*
The Roman Tragedies: *Julius Caesar, Antony and Cleopatra, Coriolanus.*

Shakespeare's tragedies have been found to be of surpassing excellence, whatever the time of the critic, or the mode of criticism. In his own time Ben Jonson loved him "this side idolatry", and this is what a modern critic says:

> Plots of desire conventionally figure woman as the erotic object but in Othello the iconic center of the spectacle is shifted from the woman to the monstrous Othello whose blackness charms and threatens, but ultimately fulfills the cultural prejudices it represents.[1]

This is written four centuries after Jonson, yet it agrees with him in finding excellence in our poet.

Reference

1. Wain, John, ed., *Shakespeare: Othello*; A Casebook, Houndmills, Palgrave, 1994. Essay by Karen Newman, p. 213.

2

The Background

(a) The Socio-Political Background

No individual, or his work, can be separated from his background and it is very necessary that the socio-political background of a writer be taken into account when a study of his work is being undertaken. Some of the relevant socio-political events of Shakespeare's time are given below in chronological order, which shall be followed by some more detailed account. Religion was one of the chiefest pre-occupations of the day and consequently the main religious events are mentioned as well as the scientific inventions. Queen Elizabeth's time was one of great geographical expansion as well as military exploits and these too are mentioned below.

A CHRONOLOGICAL TABLE

1558 – Queen Mary I dies. Elizabeth I succeeds.

– Mary Queen of Scots marries the French Dauphin. The French capture Calais.

'59 – Mary Queen of Scots declares herself the Queen of England.

– War between Spain and France ends.

– Church of England re-established more firmly.

'60 – The Scottish Parliament established the Reformed Church and breaks with Rome.

'61 – Mary Queen of Scots returns from France. She clashes with the Calvinists.

'62 – The Huguenots begin emigrating from France to England.

1563 – Bubonic plague in Europe.

'64 – *Shakespeare born*. Anglo-French war ends. England at war with Spain. Galileo born.

– The thirty-nine Articles adopted by the Church of England, Queen Elizabeth tries to enforce unity of religion.

'67 – Mary Queen of Scots abdicates. Rugby Chapel founded.

'68 – Mary Queen of Scots flees to England. She is held captive by Queen Elizabeth.

'69 – Rebellion of Roman Catholic earls crushed.

'70 – Pope Pius V excommunicates Queen Elizabeth.

'74 – Burbage gets licence to build the first permanent theatre in London.

'76 – Tycho Brahe begins his astronomical observations. Fifth French Religious war ends.

– Burbage opens the first theatre of England at Shoreditch, in London.

'77 – England makes treaty with the Dutch.

– Sir Francis Drake begins circumnavigation of the globe in the Pelican.

'80 – Sir Francis Drake completes circumnavigation.

'81 – Conversion to Roman Catholicism declared to be a treason in England.

– Galileo discovers the law of the pendulum.

'83 – Plot against the Queen.

– Humphrey Gilbert takes possession of Newfoundland, England.

'84 – Sir Walter Raleigh discovers, names and starts to colonize Virginia.

'86 – England wins the battle of Zutphan in which Sir Philip Sidney got wounded fatally.

– Plot against the Queen Mary Queen of Scots implicated and convicted of treason.

1586 – Thomas Cavendish begins the third circumnavigation of the globe.

'87 – Rose Theatre built by Henslowe.

– Mary Queen of Scots executed for treason.

'88 – Defeat of the Spanish Armada by Sir Francis Drake.

'89 – Galileo publishes the results of his experiments with falling bodies.

'92 – John Davis discovers Falkland Islands.

'93 – Absence from the church on Sundays made punishable by law.

'95 – Southwell, the mystical poet is executed for celebrating Mass.

'96 – England, France and Netherlands form alliance against Spain.

'97 – Second Spanish Armada sent against England is destroyed by a storm.

– Statutory provision for poor Relief Beggary made illegal. Transporting of convicts to colonies.

'98 – The Bodleian Library begun Globe Theatre opened.

1601 – Earl of Essex raises rebellion against the Queen and is executed.

– The East India company dispatches its first trading fleet to Sumatra.

'02 – The end of the Irish Rebellion.

– Kepler posits heliocentric theory of the universe.

– Bodleian Library opened.

'03 – Queen Elizabeth dies. Accession of James VI of Scotland as James I of England.

– Plague in England Amnesty to Irish rebels.

– Sir Walter Raleigh sentenced for treason.

– East India Company send trade mission to India.

'04 – Peace with Spain.

– Banishment of Roman Catholic priests provokes Gunpowder Plot to blow up Parliament Houses.

1604 – Acts against priests and recusants. Anglican canons made.
– Silk manufacture begins in England.
'05 – Gunpowder Plot discovered. Conspirator Guy Fawkes arrested English colonists land in Barbados.
'07 – First permanent settlement Jamestown is founded on American mainland.
'08 – Failure of plan for union land in Scotland.
'10 – Judicial decision against royal proclamations.
– Explorer Hudson sails through Hudson Bay.
'11 – Parliament dissolved.
– Land granted in northern Ireland to Scottish and English Protestants.
'12 – Alliance with German Protestant princes.
– Witches hanged at Lancashire, the last recorded executions, for heresy.
– Colonists from Virginia begin settling in Bermuda.
'13 – Princess Elizabeth marries Elector Frederick V.
– Galileo publishes his acceptance of Copernican theory.
'16 – Shakespeare dies. Sir Walter Raleigh sets forth in search of El Dorado.

It can be seen how precarious the position of Queen Elizabeth was when Shakespeare was born. Plots against her were being continually hatched at home, and there was continuous warfare with the nations abroad. It took Queen Elizabeth quite a few years to settle firmly on the throne. Mary Queen of Scots was a continual source of trouble and finally when after plotting against the queen who was, after all, her cousin, she met with the fate proper for a traitor, Queen Elizabeth was more or less secure on the throne. She was a very fine stateswoman and a good sovereign—patriotic as well as courageous. She was tolerant in her religious policies and put an end to religious controversies. G.M. Trevelyan points this out:

> In the year in which the queen succeeded her sister Mary, Puritanism was mainly a foreign doctrine imported from

> Geneva and Rhineland; when she died it was rootedly and characteristically English.[1]

Her long reign, peaceful and prosperous, helped the spirit of Anglicanism drive deep roots in the country. Again, as the same writer points out:

> At the end of her reign, it had become a real religion; its services were dear to many, after more than forty years of use in the ancient churches of England.[2]

Just as there were problems of succession in the beginning of Elizabeth's reign (Mary Queen of Scots being a strong claimant), so were the problems and speculations towards the end of her reign. This was inevitable, as she left no direct or obvious heir to the throne. But during the decades of her reign, she gave security and prosperity to her country by her wisdom and moderation.

An important feature of the time was its continuous growth and expansion. The structure of society fostered this spirit. There were class barriers, but these were accepted, not resented so there were no frictions between the classes to hamper any kind of growth. There were the feudal lords and the working classes, but there was not much oppression of the latter by the former. It was the freedom of opportunity for everyone that mattered, not equality. The kind of difference between the lord of the manor and the peasantry that existed in medieval England did not exit in Elizabethan England:

> In Tudor England, such rigid lines were rendered impossible by the number and variety of men in intermediate classes and occupations, who were closely connected, in the business and amusement of daily life, with those above and those below them in social status.... Such was the England known and approved by Shakespeare.[3]

The dignity of labour was no mere theory but proven fact. Everyone earned a fair wage for work that was done honestly and efficiently. This helped a spirit of self-reliance and self-respect grow in the mind of ordinary people.

Most of the people were responsible self-respecting members of society and as such felt responsible towards the poor and the disabled. So the Poor Law was passed for the relief of the unfortunate. The system of Justices of Peace was instituted in which influential and responsible persons were made to minister justice in minor cases. These Justices of Peace or JPs were, in their turn, controlled by the Privy Council, a higher organisation.

By this time the economical side of society also received boost as the factory system was started. This brought about industrial prosperity. Mining improved to such an extent that many metals like lead, copper, iron and tin, which had been scarce, became available. Coal became cheaper, so homes became warmer. Glass window-panes became available so homes became brighter and lighter.

The great explorer Sir Francis Drake brought national glory by his two important achievements, the circumnavigation of the globe and the defeat of the Spanish Armada. This latter was a landmark achievement for it put an end to threats from the sea. A few years later a second Armada was sent, but it perished in a storm. This acted as a national confirmation of the faith that the English were the favoured of God. These were, from every point of view, the days of prosperity, security and also of expansion G.M. Travelyan sums up:

> By the end of Elizabeth's reign not only was English commerce and finance thus reviving and expanding on a modern basis, but her ancient rivals were in rapid decline.[4]

This expansion and prosperity continued during the Jacobean Age as well. London continued to grow (it was only one square mile in area when Shakespeare arrived there) and industry flourished. One such example has been given above—silk started being manufactured in England. Not many significant changes took place during the next forty years, for those changes that did take place were political ones, not agricultural or industrial changes. When King James VI of Scotland who was a distant cousin of Queen Elizabeth, acceded to the throne of England as King James I of England. It brought about a union of the royal families of England and Scotland. The two kingdoms remained obstinately separated though the King tried very hard to bring them together. Culturally also, Scotland, though much nearer than Holland, was not so influential as the latter.

In the very first years of his reign, King James made peace with Spain, thus removing all obstacles to maritime trade. Once the seas were safe, colonization started with great vigour. Settlers from England started moving to the fabled lands of New England, Virginia, etc. The seeds of the British Empire were sown even as the Holy Roman Empire was declining. Emigrations were organised by the Virginia Company and the Massachusetts Bay Company. These pioneers were motivated by religions as well as commercial motives. Such events interest the historian. Posterity remembers one name: Shakespeare:

> His works could never have been produced in any other period than those late Elizabethan and early Jacobean times in which it was his luck to live.[5]

(b) The Literary Background

While in Italy, the spirit of the Renaissance manifested itself through painting and sculpture, in England it found its expression through literature. A whole host of gifted poets and dramatists (as well as prose-writers) were living and writing at this time. Shakespeare's work was strongly rooted in fertile soil. A chronological table is given below which takes in the main literary events of the time, the birth and death of prominent literary figures. Some influential work of the continent shall also be mentioned. It is not possible to include the numerous works that were being written, published and staged during this fruitful time. Only a few shall be mentioned. The table begins with the first performance of *Ralph Roister Doister*, ten years before our poet's birth. Shakespeare's own works are not mentioned as they will be dealt with in the right context. (*vide* Chapter 3 *infra*)

A CHRONOLOGICAL TABLE

1554 – Sir Philip Sidney and Lyly born. *Ralph Roister Doister* staged. Bandello's stories published.

1557 – Tottl's *Miscellany*. Cavendish completes the biography of Thomas Wolsey.

'58 – Kyd, Lodge, Greene, Peele born.

'61 – *Gorboduc* performed Bacon born Castiglion's. *The Courtier*.

'63 – Drayton and Donne born. Foxe's *Book of Martyrs*.

'64 – *Shakespeare*, Marlowe, Galileo born.

'66 – Gascoigne's *Supposes*. Painter's *Palace of Pleasure*, Vol. 1.

'67 – Campion and Nashe born. *Palace of Pleasure*, Vol. II.

'70 – Roger Ascham's *The Schoolmaster*.

'72 – Camoen's (Spain) *Os Lusiados*. Donne born.

'73 – Tasso's (Italian) *Aminta*.

'75 – Heywood and Tourneur born.

– *Appius and Virginia*, *Gammer Gurton's Needle* Fleming's translation of Virgil's *Bucolics*, *Georgies*.

'76 – *Paradyse of Daynty Devises*.

'77 – Holinshed's *Chronicles*. Transl. of Ovids *Epistolae Heroidum*.

'78 – Lyly's *Euphues*.

'79 – Spenser's *Shepheard's Calendar*. Lord North's transl. of Plutarch's *Lives*; Gosson's *School of Abuse*.

'80 – Montaigne's (French) *Essais* Bks I & II.

'82 – Hakluyt's *Voyages*.

'85 – Kyd's *Spanish Tragedy*.

'86 – Sir Philip Sidney dies. Lyly's Endimion.

'87 – *Tamburlaine*, Lyly's *Gallathea*. *The Misfortunes of Arthur*. Monteverdi's (Italian) *Madrigals* Bk I.

'89 – *Jew of Malta* by Marlowe. Puttenham's *Arte of English Poesie*.

'90 – *Faerie Queene* Bks I-III published Lodge's *Rosalynde*.

'91 – Sidney's *astrophel and Stella*, Peele's *Old Wives' Tale*, Marlowe's *Edward II*.

1591 – Sir John Harington's transl. of Ariosto's *Orlando Furioso* at the Queen's command.

'92 – Revised *Arcadia*, Daniel's *To Delia* (sonnets), Marlowe's *Hero and Leander*. *Arden of Fevershani* (Anon.)

'95 – Spenser's *Amoretti* (sonnet-sequence), Sidney's *Apology for Poetry*.

'98 – Francis Mere's *Palladis Tamia*.

'99 – Spenser dies. Davies's *Nosce Teipsum*.

1600 – England's *Helicon, England's Parnassus*, Jonson's *Cynthia's Revels*, Dekker's *Shoemaker's Holiday*.

'01 – Dekker and Marston's *Satiromastix*, Jonson's *Poetaster*, Marston's *What You Will*.

'03 – Dowland's *Third Book of Songs*, Heywood's *A Woman Killed with Kindness*, Jonson's *Sejanus*, Marston's *The Dutch Courtezan*.

'04 – Chapman's *Bussy D'Ambois*, Marston's *The Malcontent*.

'05 – Drayton's *Collected Poems*, Bacon's *Advancement of Learning*, collaborated play *Eastward Ho*! Middleton's *A Trick to Catch the Old One*.

'06 – Lyly dies. *Yorkshire Tragedy* (Anon.), Jonson's *Volpone*, Tourneur's *The Revenger's Tragedy*.

'07 – Beaumont and Fletcher's *Knight of the Burning Pestle*.

'08 – Fuller and Milton born. Fletcher's *The Faithful Shepherdess*, Chapman's *Duke of Byron*.

'09 – Beaumont and Fletcher's *Philaster*, Fulke Greville's *Mustapha*, Tourneur's *Atheist's Tragedy*.

'10 – Donne's *Pseudo-Martyr*, Jonson's *The Alchemist*.

'11 – Spenser's *Collected Works*, *The Authorised Version of the Bible*, *A King and No King*.

'12 – Crashaw born. Chapman's *Iliad* I-XXIV, Donne's *Second Anniversaries*, Drayton's *Poly-Olbion*, Webster's *The White Devil*.

1613 – Constable and Overbury die. Purchas's *Pilgrimage.*
'14 – Overbury's *Characters*. Lodge's *Works of Seneca.*
'15 – Sir Walter Raleigh's *History of the World*, Jonson's *Bartholomew Fair*, Webster's *The Duchess of Malfi.*
'16 – *Shakespeare Dies*. Jonson given royal pension. Chapman's *Whole Works of Homer*. Jonson's *Works.*

As this table shows the few years from Sidney's birth in 1554 to Shakespeare's death in 1616 cover the best time of literary efflorescence in England. The most familiar names of the Elizabethan and Jacobean times come later than Sidney. The Tudor dynasty had a rose as its emblem and if the literature of the Renaissance is compared with a rose then it can be said that what Sidney saw in his lifetime was only a bud which later opened out to spread out unequalled beauty and fragrance.

Drama, the glory of the Elizabethan and Jacobean era, had barely started in Sidney's time. The plays that were being written and performed were as nothing to those that Shakespeare and others were to write, but it cannot be denied that that prepared the ground for the followers. It is not surprising that Sidney condemned contemporary drama, except for Gorboduc which he praised:

> Our tragedies and comedies not without cause cried out against, observing rules neither of honest civility nor of skilful poetry: excepting *Gorboduc* (again I say of those that I have seen), which notwithstanding as it is full of stately speeches and well-sounding phrases, climbing to the height of Seneca's style, and as full of no-table morality, which it doth most delightfully teach, and so obtain the very end of poesy.[6]

Gorboduc, to-day, has more of a historical interest than as a work of great literary merit. Sidney praised it because there was nothing superior to it. *Ralph Roister Doister* and rollicking comedy had been staged ten years before Shakespeare's birth. *The Misfortunes of Arthur*, a play in the nature of a history, had been written for the Queen's entertainment in 1587. These works have only historical importance today and cannot by any means be considered seriously as works of great merit.

The prospect is a little better than drama when we turn to narrative poetry, songs and sonnets, all of which Shakespeare wrote. Spenser's *Shepheards Calendar* and parts of *Faerie Queene* had been published before Shakespeare's own narrative poems. Tottel had published his famous *Miscellany* which included the sonnets of Wyatt and Surrey. The famous sequences of Elizabethan love-sonnet started being written by the end of the sixteenth century, reaching their climax in Shakespeare's sequence. The most flourishing genre was that of the lyric. The best lyrics were written by the "Elizabethan nest of singing-birds" from 1580 to 1620, and were being collected and published.

Shakespeare's plays are full of songs and in writing them he took the help of these collections, adapting the words to suit his own requirements. These were mostly light-hearted love-songs:

> The song-lyric, as developed in accord with musical art of the time, is too light an instrument to utter the deeper notes of passion and its theme is fanciful love.[7]

As the Elizabethan Age advanced, the output became more and more prolific as well as dazzling. Lyric poetry, narrative poetry, discursive poetry—all flourished in a manner hardly equalled before or since. Prose, which is of minor importance to us (only as the sources of Shakespeare's plays) was developed not only in the romances of Sidney, Lyly and others, but also in the philosophical works of writers like Bacon, Hooker, Sir Thomas Brown et al.

It is drama which is the most important of the literary genres for our present purposes. The university wits took London by storm by starting with Kyd's *The Spanish Tragedy*, a revenge tragedy in the Senecan mode which was all the rage. This became the archetype for all revenge tragedies. Marlowe's very first attempt *Tamburlaine* (a conqueror tragedy) became so popular that he quickly wrote the second part of the play. As theatres were established, by Burbage and Henslowe, plays were in great demand. The dramatists had ample opportunity for experimenting with different kinds of plays and finding the form that suited them. Shakespeare was specially versatile and no one could rival him in the range of his plays or otherwise, but each of the playwrights could find and settle down with the form that suited them the best, as Ben Jonson did with his humour comedies and Beaumont and Fletcher with their tragic-comedies.

The dramatists were highly influenced by classical writers. Seneca for example was a prevailing influence. Kyd set the example.

> It was the genius of Thomas Kyd that seized upon the essential effects of Senecan action and adapted them, with much relaxation of rules, to the conditions of the public stage.[8]

F.T. Bowers has categorized these tragedies, known as the Blood-and-thunder tragedies, into four divisions: Conqueror tragedy (*Tamburlaine, Macbeth,* etc.), Revenge tragedy (*The Spanish Tragedy*, *Halmet,* etc.), Villain tradegy (*The Changeling, Othello,* etc.), and Domestic tragedy (*A Woman Killed with Kindness*, *Romeo and Juliet,* etc.). There are many tragedies that cannot be contained within just one group. Webster's *The Duchess of Malfi* for example, is a revenge tragedy as well as a domestic tragedy. Shakespeare's *Othello* is a villain tragedy as well as a domestic tragedy.

Comedy too, flourished in the hands of Lyly, Peele, Greene, Shakespeare, Ben Jonson and others. M.C. Bradbrook has divided Elizabethan society into three categories, the Court, the Country and the City, and ascribes different kinds of comedy to each. The comedies of Shakespeare come mostly under the first of these and those of Ben Jonson under the third. There is great variety within this kind of play. There are Romantic comedies like those written by Shakespeare, Satirical comedies like those of Ben Jonson, Problem comedies like the four written by Shakespeare, Tragic-comedies like those by Beaumont and Fletcher, and Romances like the last plays of Shakespeare.

Numerous masques were also used for courtly entertainment. Those of Ben Jonson were specially successful. Shakespeare used the device quite frequently in his plays.

Shakespeare's works thus, were firmly rooted into the soil of Elizabethan England and he is the ideal product of his milieu. Another poet centuries later, points out the relevance of the background:

> No poet, no artist of any art, has his complete meaning alone. His significance, his appreciation is the appreciation of his relation to the dead poets and artists.[9]

References

1. Trevelyan, G.M., *Illustrated English Social History*, Vol. 2, Harmondsworth, Penguin Book Ltd., 1964, p. 86.
2. *Ibid.*
3. *Ibid.*, p. 62.
4. *Ibid.*, p. 23.
5. *Ibid.*, p. 125.
6. Enright, D.J. and Chickera, Ernst de, ed., *English Critical Texts: 16th Century to 20th Century*, Oxford, the University Press, 2002, p. 40.
7. Carpenter, Frederick Ives, *English Lyric Poetry: 1500-1700*, London, Blackie & Son Ltd., no date, p. xlvii.
8. Craig, Hardin, *The Literature of the English Renaissance*: 1485-1660. New York, Collier Books, 1962, p. 80.
9. Eliot, T.S., *Three Essays*, Calcutta, Oxford University Press, 1979, p. 17.

3

Life and Works

(a) A Short Biography

Many biographies of Shakespeare have been written but, all the same, a lot of the details as supplied therein are not very dependable. There are many anecdotes about him but they are more like legends than historical facts, particularly those related to his early days. Details about his later life, specially those from the time that his group became accepted at Court, are historically true and fully reliable. As usually happens in the case of well-known figures, Shakespeare also became invested with an aura of glory, all the more pronounced as this renown was not posthumous but attained during his lifetime. In the seventeenth century. Fuller wrote a brief life in his famous *Worthies* (1662) and John Aubrey in his *Lives of Eminent Men* included him. The first modern editor Nicholas Rowe took material from many other sources as well in the life given in his edition of the plays. More intensive research has been done by modern biographers. More material is available on him than on his other contemporaries. A chronological table of the chief events of his life is being given, followed by a short biography.

A CHRONOLOGICAL TABLE OF THE CHIEF EVENTS OF HIS LIFE

1564 – Apr. 23, the supposed date of birth of Shakespeare.

– Apr. 26, Shakespeare christened at the local parish church of Stratford-upon-Avon.

'71 – Possible time of enrolment in the local school.

'78 – His father's fortunes undergo reverses and he is,

possibly, withdrawn from school at this time, or perhaps later.

1582 – Shakespeare gets married to Anne Hathaway.

'83 – Birth of Susanna, his first child.

'85 – The twins, Hamnet and Judith, are born.

'86 – Shakespeare's supposed departure for London.

'93 – *Venus and Adonis* published by Richard Field.

'94 – *Rape of Lucrece* pub. *Titus Andronicus* staged. *The Taming of the Shrew.*[1]

'95 – *A Midsummer Night's Dream.*

,96 – Death of Hamnet his only son. *Sonnets.*

'97 – Shakespeare buys New Place. *The Merchant of Venice.*

'99 – He buys shares in the Globe Theatre. *Much Ado, As You Like It, Twelfth Night, Henry V, Julius Caesar.*

1602 – The birth of his first grandchild. He buys one hundred and seven acres of land. *All's well that Ends well, Troilus* and *Cressida, Hamlet.*

'04 – His company taken under royal patronage and given the name of the King's Men. *Measure for Measure, Othello.*

'05 – *Macbeth.*

'06 – *King Lear.*

'07 – *Timon of Athens.*

'09 – *Coriolanus. Sonnets* published.

'11 – He retires from the company and comes back to his native village. *The Winter's Tale, The Tempest.*

'12 – *Henry VIII.*

'16 – His Last will and Testament drawn up.

– Apr. 23. Shakespeare dies on his fifty-second birth anniversary.

– Apr. 25. He is buried in the chancel of the Stratford Church.

The exact date of his birth is not known, as the Register of Baptism maintained by the parish church did not record the date of birth but of baptism only. As the official language of the time was Latin, the entry in the Register says:

1564, Apr. 26, Gulielmus Filius Johannes Shakespere.[2]

It was the custom those days to baptize a baby three days after its birth, perhaps because of the prevalence of infant mortality. It is, therefore, assumed that he was born on the twenty-third of April, in the village of Stratford-upon-Avon, the county being Warwickshire. This was a lucky day for it was St. George's day, England's patron saint.

Not much is known about his childhood days but it can be taken for granted that he spent a happy and secure childhood in the bosom of a loving and prosperous family. His position in the family was a significant one as he was the eldest son. His father John Shakespeare was in the trade and therefore not regarded as a gentleman (i.e., belonging to the class of landed gentry), but was a worthy man in society. Later, he was to become the alderman for by this time the little village had expanded enough to have one. This was in 1565 and by this time he was in a position to claim the status of a gentleman. Keeping in mind the feudal structure of contemporary society, this fact was of great significance. Socially speaking, Shakespeare's mother came from a family belonging to a higher level, for Mary Arden's father belonged to the class of small landed gentry.

The village was surrounded by a wonderful countryside, and William, as a little boy, would run wild in the lap of benevolent Nature. The memory of this beautiful environment was to produce the lovely and lyrical passages of nature description in his poetry. The sunny glades of the Forest of Arden look back to these joyful experiences, though, of course, Shakespeare mentions the freezing skies and the bitter wind of winter as well. For he was not one to shirk the reality.

Another significant fact is that his father was a Justice of Peace (*vide* Chapter 2, *supra*) as well as the High Bailiff of Stratford. He had to execute many duties connected with courts of law and Shakespeare, being the eldest son, often accompanied him. He thus gained intimate knowledge of legal procedures, of which the trial scene of *The Merchant of Venice* is the proof.

Queen Elizabeth had established Grammar Schools all over England in order to educate the commoners. Shakespeare was duly admitted to the local one. He was perhaps seven at this time and did not take kindly to it at all. It is, therefore, thought that in the passage in *As You Like It* where Jaques refers to the school-boy, Shakespeare is referring to himself, or, at least, writing out of personal experience:

> Then the whining school-boy, with his satchel
> And shining morning face, creeping like snail
> Unwillingly to school.[3]

Latin grammar was the most important part of the curriculum in these schools. Boys of the aristocratic class went to exclusive and expensive schools where they got classical education which Shakespeare could not get. But this does not mean that he did not get any education in the classics. Ben Jonson's ridicule of his "small Latin and less Greek" is well-known but most misleading. Shakespeare may not have been a classical scholar of a good standard according to contemporary expectations, but he had acquired a fair knowledge of classical literature. Shakespeare was a student here till he was about 14 or 16, it is not known exactly when he left the school.

All these schools in England followed the same curriculum and kept the same hours. School started at six in the morning and went on till five in the evening. There were breaks during the day and there were clear-cut rules which laid down that, in all, there had to be two and a half hours' break spaced out during the day. The curriculum is given below:

Poetry : *The Bucolica* of Mantuan.
The Eclogues and *The Aeneid* of Virgil.
The Poems of Horace.
The Metamorphoses of Ovid.
Prose: Caesar, Livy, Cicero.
Drama: Ten tragedies of Seneca.
The comedies of Plautus.
The comedies of Terence.

This makes it quite clear that Shakespeare had a solid foundation of classical education. The classical references that occur continuously in his play come from first-hand knowledge of classical literature. One of his biographers' remarks:

> Today all scholars are agreed that Shakespeare was a well-educated man of his times, that he certainly continued to further his education by wide reading throughout his life and that there is no display of learning in any one of his plays which could not have been acquired at the Stratford Grammar School.[4]

There is another opinion that goes totally against this idea of Shakespeare's schooling. It is a well-known fact that the family was a Catholic one and, basing his theory on this fact, John Dover Wilson has argued that John Shakespeare may not have put his son in the Grammar School at all. There were many great Catholic noblemen at the time and he might have sent his son to one such household. Shakespeare might have received his education and gained inside knowledge of the lifestyle of the aristocracy in this manner and depicted it in his plays.

After some years, some kind of misfortune had visited the family and John Shakespeare's fortunes went under an eclipse. Shakespeare was taken out of the school in his teens, but it is not known exactly when. It is not known whether he had completed his education by that time either. Every year, every hour of education is of crucial importance at this age, for the mind is more capable of learning at this time than at any other. How much harm it has done to Shakespeare's future career is only to be guessed at.

It was during these highly formative years that Shakespeare first came into contact with stage-performances. Many records exist of different traveling companies of players visiting his village. These itinerant groups were patronized by the great aristocrats of the time and were accordingly named after them. There were groups belonging to the Earls of Leicester, Warwick and Worcester. They staged the traditional moralities as well as the modern five-act plays written in imitation of classical models, like *Gorboduc,* etc.

While still in his teens, Shakespeare's sensitive and young mind fell to charms of the local belle Anne Hathaway from a village that lay at a little distance, named Shottery. She was a much admired and sought after girl, as becomes clear from, an anonymous couplet often quoted by his biographers:

Anne Hathaway, she hath a way
To charm all hearts, Anne Hathaway.

Young Shakespeare was the one on whom she bestowed her favours and agreed to marry. She was eight years older than him but this was no barrier to the lovers and they got married on Nov. 28, 1582. He was not yet nineteen, whereas she was twenty-six. Next year Susanna, their first child, was born. She was baptized on May 26, 1583. Nearly two years later, the twins, Hamnet and Judith, were born. Hamnet died in 1596, leaving no one to carry on the line.

Thus, when barely twenty-one, Shakespeare was a man with three children, a wife eight years older than himself and no visible means of earning a livelihood. Nor was his father's financial position at all an enviable one. There are many versions of how he earned a livelihood at this time. John Aubrey, one of the first biographers in English, had recorded that he was teaching in a school near his own village. How far this is true is debatable. Another better-known story is given by a clergyman and the actor Thomas Betterton. This story became so widely known that it is commonly accepted as true, though it is highly debatable how much of truth there is in it. At Charlecote, there was a deer park which was the property of one Sir Thomas Lucy. It was said that Shakespeare, along with some other young men, stole a deer from this park. They were all caught and it is said that Sir Thomas had ordered the young men to be whipped and put into prison. It is also said that Shakespeare resented this bitterly and took his revenge on Sir Thomas portraying him as Justice Shallow, the stupid judge in *The Merry Wives of Windsor*, and *Henry IV*. Modern researches however, have proved that this story is of doubtful authenticity, for Sir Thomas was not the master of Charlecote forest at that time. It has, however, been supposed for a long time that it was this humiliation that acted as a deciding factor behind Shakespeare's leaving Stratford, in 1586, for London.

Another legend connected with this time of Shakespeare's life, is that he had joined one of the itinerant dramatic companies as an actor, spending quite a few years with it. Again, no one is sure of how much of truth there is in this story. What has given rise to it is a will left by a rich Lancashire gentleman, leaving a considerable sum to one William Shakeshafte, a player in his service. This name is suggestive, for Shakeshafte is variant of the surname Shakespeare. Such variants were common in Elizabethan times, for English was as yet a fluid, young language, with its grammar and pronunciation not yet rigidly formulated.

It is known for sure that the dramatic group, the Queen's Men, visited Stratford at this time, and perhaps this made Shakespeare's thoughts turn towards London. Many other groups also came there and Shakespeare had become familiar with theatrical productions while still young. In 1583, for example, three well-known groups produced plays at Stratford. Two famous and well-organized groups had come there in 1587. Many of his biographers think that he had acted in these. Hamlets's well-known conversation with the players gives evidence of first-hand knowledge not only of acting but of stagecraft as well.

The period stretching from 1586 to 1592 is known as the Dark Years, for little is known of them. As the true facts are non-existent, anecdotes exist in great profusion. It is said that he would be loitering outside the playhouses in order to earn a little money by looking after the horses of the gentlemen who came riding to watch the plays. Another legend has it that he was a prompter's assistant. What is known for sure is that he had found a fellow villager named Richard Field who had left Stratford before Shakespeare did and had become an established printer by this time.

This friend published his *Venus and Adonis* in 1593 and *The Rape of Lucrece* the next year, both of which became instantly popular. His literary career, thus, had begun with narrative poems which were very popular at this time.

In the field of drama, his only serious rival at this time was Marlowe, and it is a remarkable coincidence that the two of them, each independently had reached London at the same time. The two chronological tables given above show that they had been born the same year also. This decade (the eighties) was a highly prosperous and stimulating one. Sir Francis Drake was scouring the Spanish Main and Sir Philip Sidney was in the process of writing the first sequence love-sonnets, *Astrophel and Stella*. Perhaps his monumental prose romance *Arcadia*, also, was being drafted at the same time. Out in Ireland, Spenser was composing his poetical masterpiece, *The Faerie Queene*. One by one the members of the group of learned young men, the University Wits, were converging towards London. Lyly, the leader of the group, had already produced his *Euphues* and was now turning towards drama. Two of his romantic comedies, *Campaspe* and *Sappho and Phaon* for the Queen by the choir of the Chapel Royal in 1584. It was *Euphues*, that brought him fame. It was so popular with the ladies that Lyly has declared the hope that:

> Euphues had rather lie shut in a Lady's casket than open on a scholar's study.[5]

London, in other words, was the center of cultural and other activities. Marlowe's *Tamburlaine* was presented in 1587, and by then Shakespeare was definitely present there. It was a truly wonderful time of expansion and therefore of enthusiasm, with horizons receding farther and farther in every field. This was the London to which Shakespeare came, F.E. Halliday remarks:

> Shakespeare had arrived in London at the most thrilling moment in its history; thrilling, however, not only because of danger, anxiety, expectation and hope in the air, but also because the long-awaited dramatic revival was now imminent.[6]

Shakespeare watched and avidly learned from, the plays that were being staged, perhaps acting minor parts in them. He must have been consolidating his position in literary London slowly but surely because his works had become important enough to be noticed by such a well-established University wit as Greene. It is he who is always cited as being the first contemporary to have mentioned Shakespeare's name. It occurs, in a pamphlet remembered today chiefly for this reason, named *Greene's Groats-worth of Wit bought with a Million of Repentance*. At the end of this, there is a letter addressed to

Peele, Nashe and, of course, Marlowe. He warns them against actors, particularly against a certain actor, in a highly allusive manner. There can be no doubt that the reference is to Shakespeare whom he ridicules and castigates in offensive terms:

> Yes, trust them not; for there is an upstart crow, beautified with our feathers that with his Tyger's heart wrapt in a Player's hyde, supposes he is as well able to bombast out a blank verse as the best of you: and being an absolute Johannes factotum, is in his own conceit, the only shake-scene in a country.[7]

Two clear clues indicate our poet in this famous sentence. The line "Tyger's heart wrapt in a player's hyde" is a deliberate misquotation of Shakespeare's line "o tiger's heart wrapped in a woman's hide" in *Henry VI, pt. III.* Next there is the word "shake-scene" which is a sarcastic reference to our poet's name. This kind of reference speaks volumes about Greene's spitefulness and jealousy, but also makes it clear that by this time Shakespeare had become important enough to cause alarm to the reigning dramatists. This reference occurred in 1592 and from now onwards there are frequent bits of information on him. To have made a mark in six years is no mean achievement for the ignorant country yokel as he must have appeared to the sophisticated and well-established University Wits.

At this time, he was still learning his craft and these years are known as the years of apprenticeship. He was, however, not merely learning, but producing also. The sonnet-sequence to Mr. W.H., the two narrative poems, *The Henry VI* trilogy, *Richard III*, *Titus Andronicus*, *The Comedy of Errors*, *The Two Gentlemen of Verona* and *The Taming of the Shrew* were all churned out at this time. They were all highly successful. It seems surprising today that an unsubtle blood-and-thunder tragedy like *Titus Andronicus* was so popular in its day that it was published in 1594 and the title-page reveals its success:

> ...as it was played by the Rt. Hon. the Earl of Derby, the Earl of Pembroke and the Earl of Sussex their servants.[8]

These three were all well-known companies. It is also clear that they had put it up in quick succession.

The list given above is significant also as it shows that Shakespeare had not confined his talent to any particular genre. Kyd and Marlowe had written only tragedies. Shakespeare, from the very beginning, was able to produce successful comedies (*The Two Gentlemen of Verona*), tragedies (*Titus Andronicus*) and histories in the field of drama itself, let alone that of sonnets and poems. Marlowe had already been killed by 1594 and Shakespeare had proved his versatility as well as stage-worthiness.

By this time he had joined the group of Lord Chamberlaine's Men, and had become an important member of it. This can be surmised because at this time the company had produced two plays at Court and the receipt of payment issued by the Royal Treasury contains the names of Shakespeare, Kempe and Burbage. Shakespeare remained in this company till the very end of his life. It was a case of a very happy symbiosis, for a company needed a good writer of its own in order to be in a state of continuous productivity, and a writer, of course, needed a company to produce his plays.

It is thought that he had paid a visit to Stratford at this time. Shakespeare's father, now in his sixties, was the head of a big family, surrounded by his children and grandchildren. Shakespeare himself was twenty-eight and his children were growing up—Susanna was nine and the twins were seven. It was time for Hamnet to start school. Shakespeare stayed in the bosom of his family for four months and it is thought that he wrote *Richard III* and *Venus and Adonis* during this visit. The poem was dedicated to the Earl of Southampton, the supposed "onlie begetter" of the sonnet-sequence.

Shakespeare was lucky to find a patron like the young Earl of Southampton, a handsome aristocrat about ten years junior to himself. He was a well-known patron of arts and, soon enough, a deep and intense friendship developed between them. The sonnets speak eloquently of this relationship, though there is no way of proving it in any other way. The Earl, not named anywhere in the sequence, is designated as Mr. W.H. in the Dedication and it is thought that these are the initial of Henry Wriothesley (the Earl of Southempton) in reversed order. The sonnets also describe a nameless Dark Lady with whom

Shakespeare was in love. There follows a harrowing account of how Mr. W.H. and the Dark Lady together betrayed Shakespeare. How much of this is true cannot be known for sure but Shakespeare's intense love for Mr. W.H. is quite apparent. It has been expressed in the passionate tradition of Courtly Love.

Though the story told by the sonnets may not have much biographical relevance, it is quite true that Shakespeare enjoyed the patronage of the Earl of Southampton. He had dedicated the two narrative poems in addition to the sonnets to his patron. The Dedication in *The Rape of Lucrece* is instinct with the worshipful adoration he had towards Mr. W.H.:

> The love I dedicate to your Lordship is without end... What I have done is yours, what I have to do is yours, being part in all I have devoted yours.[9]

The patronage of the Earl gave his life the security that is so necessary for an artist. He was able to buy a share in his own company—the money; it is believed, being supplied by the Earl. In those times, a poet had to have patronage in order to survive, unless, of course, he had some other source of income. Shakespeare was fortunate indeed. At this time, Greene was languishing in poverty and sickness, whereas Shakespeare was buying property. A.L. Rowse remarks:

> It meant all the difference between the dreadful insecurity poor Greene had, and others, died of, and having firm ground under his feet.[10]

His company having him for its writer soon became the leading company in London. Apart from public performances; it gave thirty-two stagings in Queen Elizabeth's Court, a rare distinction for any theatrical company.

How prosperous and successful Shakespeare was can be understood only if we take a look at the literary perspective of the time. First of all, he was the only dramatist to survive the terrible havoc wrought by the Plague. Kyd was already dead at thirty-five years of age and Marlowe who was his most serious rival, was killed suddenly at a drunken brawl. Greene was dead at thirty-four years, and Peele would die in a few years. Lyly and Lodge had almost come to the end of their productivity. Nashe had turned to pamphlets in preference to plays. Ben Jonson, the only dramatist of a caliber like his own, had still not come. Shakespeare's star was in the ascendant at the moment.

The highly entertaining early comedies now poured forth. A successful man-about-town, he was enjoying life to the full and it is thought that Lord Berowne, the gayest and wittiest Lord in *Love's Labour's Lost* is, as Halliday describes, "a half-mocking and unconscious projection of himself". This was the year of 1595, and he was thirty years old, in the full vigour of energetic creativity. A literary mention of his name occurs in poem by an Oxford undergraduate, one Henry Willoughby. He mentions Shakespeare as one who gives good advice about love affairs. The poet particularly mentions his narrative poem:

> Yet Tarquin plucked his glistering grape
> And Shakespeare paints poor Lucrece's rape.[11]

In 1597, Shakespeare had the tragic experience of losing his only son and heir Hamnet. He was writing *King John* at the time. His father had, earlier, applied at the Herald's College for a coat-of-arms without any success and Shakespeare now pursued the matter. This would give his family the status of a gentleman—a matter of great importance in the feudal society of the time. This time the request was granted and our poet came back to London as a gentleman. He also bought New Place which was the second best house in Stratford, the first being the Town Hall. Stratford was no longer a little village, it had expanded into a big enough place to require a Town Hall. This gives an idea of Shakespeare's status.

By 1598, he was acknowledged as a master dramatist. A well-known document of the time named *Palladis Tamia* written by Francis Meres gives a eulogistic account of his works:

> ...the sweet wittie soule of Ovid lives in mellifluous and hony-tongued Shakespeare, witness his *Venus and Adonis*, his *Lucrece*, his surged sonnets among his friends.[12]

This work gives a list of the plays that had been written and staged to date. This list is of great help to scholars in determining the dates of his works. Meres's attitude is a pointer to the high esteem in which Shakespeare was held. He asserts that Shakespeare is the contemporary equivalent of Terence and Plautus in comedy and of Seneca in tragedy.

Not only was Shakespeare acclaimed as the best dramatist of the time, but his company also got recognition. The Queen passed away in 1603 and King James VI of Scotland acceded to the throne of England as King James I. He took the Lord Chamberlaine's Men under his own patronage and the company was named as the King's Men. This was a coveted position—in fact the highest honour for any group. The members of the company would have the royal livery to wear and take part in all royal pageants and processions.

There are many records of Shakespeare's life from this point onwards. He had become well-settled in London. Legal documents prove that he went on changing his dwelling place, staying at Bishop Gate in 1595, at Southwark in 1599, at Cripplegate in 1604. He bought a house at Blackfriars in 1613 though he did not occupy it. In 1602, he acquired a hundred and seven acres of land for farming and later in the same year, he bought a cottage and a quarter acre of land. He continued to write for his company and also acted in it, for there exists a record that showed he had acted in Ben Jonson's *Sejanus*, a historical tragedy performed by his company in 1603.

He returned to Stratford in 1603 when there was another plague in London. His great tragedies were now produced. *Hamlet* was staged in 1602—the last play he wrote in the Elizabethan Age. In 1604 Othello, the first of his Jacobean plays was performed at Court. The Chronicles and the Problem plays were all written in the Jacobean Age. There is a great difference in spirit between the Elizabethan and the Jacobean Age. As Theodore Spencer has pointed out, the Renaissance optimism was succeeded by the Jacobean Age of conflict and pessimism. A sombre evaluation of life and person succeeded exuberance and enthusiasm. As Theodore Spencer has remarked:

> The earlier Renaissance had emphasized man's potentialities by comparing man with the angels; the later

> Renaissance emphasized their destruction by comparing man with the animals.[13]

The plays Shakespeare wrote at this time reflect this sombre attitude. The tragedies and the problems plays reflect the very spirit of the age in that they reflect upon the spirit of man and the nature of evil.

By now Shakespeare was spending his summers regularly at Stratford. In 1608, his mother passed away and his first grandchild was born. Both of these are events of moment, signifying the onset of age. In three more years (1611), he would leave London and settle at Stratford.

As the years passed, he left the turbulent waters of the problem comedies and the tragedies behind him and emerged into the deep serenity of the last romances. The sonnet-sequence was published in 1609 and in 1611 (according to Irving Ribner and others), he retired to Stratford.

His connections with London, however, were not severed. He continued coming there on matters of business. For example, he got the Blackfriar Gate House in 1613, and his name continued to appear in various documents. He kept his connections with the stage for at the end of 1612. *The Tempest* was performed to celebrate a royal betrothal. It is said that he himself enacted the role of Prospero and blessed the couple.

His health was failing, though it is not well-known what he was suffering from. In 1616, his will was drawn up and can still be seen in Somerset House. This was in February and two months later, on 23rd April which was his birthday, he passed away at fifty-four years of age.

Many rich and complex symbols adorn his grave. There is a bust of him with quill in his hand, signifying that he was a writer. Corinthian columns stand at the sides with a cornice on them. The allegorical figures of Rest and of Labour adorn this cornice. His coat-of-arms is placed between these two figures and the whole thing is surmounted by a skull. There is a memorial tablet with a Latin couplet and a sextet in English. The grave itself bears an epitaph in the form of a quatrain. It is thought that this was written by the poet himself, though many scholars think that it is a bit too crude to have been his own work. This is how it runs:

> Good friend, for Jesus sake forbeare
> To dig the dust enclosed here!
> Blest be the man yt spares these stones,
> And curst be he yt moves my bones.[14]

(b) Shakespeare's Works

A tentative scheme of Shakespeare's works has been drawn up by his critics and biographers. This has been based on contemporary documents like Henslowe's *Diary*, the Stationer's Register and others. These recorded the dates of the performances on stage, not of composition or of publications. Again, the dates of performances of many plays are not known and to make the whole thing even more confusing, some of the plays like *Titus Andronicus* were published quite early, and some much later. Notwithstanding these difficulties, a scheme has been more or less agreed upon, though the stages cannot really be strictly demarcated.

Phase I

1591 – *The Comedy of Errors.*

'92 – *The Two Gentlemen of Verona*, *Henry VI*, *Parts I, II and III.*

'93 – *King Richard III*, *Romeo and Juliet*, *Venus and Adonis.*

Phase II

1594 – *The Rape of Lucrece*, *The Sonnets*, *Titus Andronicus*, *King Richard II*, *A Midsummer Night's Dream*, *Love's Labour's Lost*, *King John*, *The Taming of the Shrew.*

'95 – *The Merchant of Venice.*

'97 – *Henry IV, pt. I.*

'98 – *Henry IV, pt. II*, *The Merry Wives of Windsor.*

'99 – *Henry V*, *Much Ado About Nothing*, *Julius Caesar.*

1600 – *As You Like It*, *Twelfth Night.*

Phase III

1602 – *Hamlet, Troilus and Cressida, All's Well That Ends Well.*

'04 – *Measure for Measure, Othello.*

'05 – *King Lear.*

'06 – *Macbeth.*

'07 – *Antony and Cleopatra.*

'08 – *Coriolanus, Timon of Athens, Pericles.*

Phase IV

1610 – *Cymbeline, The Winter's Tale, The Tempest.*

'11 – *Henry VIII.*

As this table shows, Shakespeare's career has been divided into four phases, though these are not mutually exclusive. Some critics, for example, think that all the works up to *Love's Labour's Lost* belong to the first phase, while some say that *Pericles* belongs to the fourth phase, not the third. These are matters of opinion. The first phase in known as the phase of Experiment or of Apprenticeship, from 1591 to 1594 or perhaps to 1595. At this time, he was busy re-writing or revising plays that were already in existence—the best way for learning one's craft. He made frequent use of couplets and end-stopped lines at this time, as can be seen, for example, in *A Midsummer Night's Dream*. Exuberant word-play can be seen in *Love's Labour's Lost*. The art of characterisation has not developed yet, though he balances his characters against each other quite expertly.

The period of Development stretches from 1594-95 to 1601. He produced the Golden comedies (of which *As You Like It* is thought to be the best) and the Chronicles during this time. He has attained mastery over blank verse and has started to plumb the depths of the human mind in his portrayal of characters. The plots too, are handled with expertise.

1608 saw the end of the third phase. One can see a definite change of attitude in the work of this period. The witty and light-hearted characters are no longer there. Instead, he has started looking evil in the face, evil in humanity as well as in Nature:

> The conflict between good and evil, ugliness and beauty, innocence and crime, purity and impurity, hope and disgust, love and hate, order and disorder, natural laws and the anarchy produced by the passions—all is resolved in Shakespeare's so-called "dark period" with an infinite despair.[15]

The Problem comedies and the Great tragedies belong to this period.

From now till 1612 is the last phase or the Romance period during which the last four Romances were written. Shakespeare has now achieved the wisdom that comes with age, a calm acceptance of the presence of evil as inevitable and looking forward to the future with hope that a new generation will create a better world. Fluchère remarks:

> As his career draws to a close Shakespeare turned back to his youth, and his implicit theme is always that of fertility resurrection, joy of life.[16]

The four Romances were followed by two more plays. Even up till the twentieth century, there had been controversy about the chronicle play *King Henry VIII*. Nowadays, however, scholars agree in ascribing it to him. The *Two Noble Kinsmen*, it has always been known, was work of collaboration with Fletcher.

The time has now come to cast a passing glance at his works. In the brief notes on his plays and poems that shall now be given, it has been tried to follow a roughly chronological order. As the dates of composition, performance and publication differ, it is difficult if not impossible, to be exact.

(c) Brief Notes on His Works

The Comedy of Errors

This play is his shortest, and was staged in 1594. There are many critics who think this to be the first of his works. The plot is from Plautus's rollicking comedy, *The Menaechmuses* in which there is but one pair of twins and Shakespeare has doubled this. Consequently, the intrigues as well as the cases of mistaken identities have multiplied. The only theme that takes prominence is that of the relationship between husband and wife, which Shakespeare will deal with in detail later on, in *The Taming of the Shrew*.

The Two Gentlemen of Verona

This play is usually looked upon as the first of his romantic comedies. There are two pairs of lovers, two servants and two fathers. The characters, thus, are balanced against each other and make a symmetrical pattern. Conflict between love and friendship is the theme and the emphasis falls on friendship. There is also the theme of forgiveness and reconciliation that will occupy the poet so intensely in the last romances. Many features of his mature comedies, like crossed love disguised heroines, exile, flight, etc. appear in this play. Julia is a precursor of Rosalind and Portia, and Silvia of Juliet.

Henry VI, Pts. I, II & III

This trilogy begins the chronicles that brought Shakespeare so much renown. He wrote ten such plays, including *Henry VIII*. These are not mere records of historical events. The serious issues of the duties and privileges of Kings are also dealt with. He presented their human as well as ceremonial aspects, with all the pomp and pageantry it involved.

These plays were staged in 1592 and became so popular that the entire trilogy was performed three times in eight days. Greene had referred to one of the lines (*vide* Chapter 2, *supra*). It presents a world of ferocity and ends in regicide.

Richard III

The early poetry of Shakespeare shows the influence of Marlowe. The Henry VI trilogy showed this quite clearly and in this play the influence can be seen not only in poetry but in characterisation as well. Richard III the hero, is a Marlovian figure and the play too, is more like a tragedy than a history play. It is the second longest play of Shakespeare and extremely effective on the stage. Many critics group this play with the *Henry VI* trilogy and call the entire sequence a tetralogy. Yet the figure of the

King dominates the play and his woeful fate makes the plays a tragedy, evoking pity and terror.

Romeo and Juliet

This is one of his most popular tragedies telling the story of star-crossed lovers. The hero and the heroine have become the archetypes of unfortunate lovers. This, like the Greek tragedies, is a tragedy of fate, with family feud taking the place of fate. Shakespeare has not yet perfected his art of characterisation to the extent when it can be said that in his tragedies character is destiny. Instead, he has followed the original story very closely. Some of the speeches and scenes in it have become classics, particularly the Queen Mab speech by Merutio and the Balcony scene between the lovers.

Venus and Adonis

Narrative poems based on classical myths were very popular and Shakespeare's became an instant hit. He took the story from Ovid, and the poem ran through ten or eleven editions in his own lifetime. He had many good models before him, particularly those by the University Wits. Narrative poetry was new genre for him, but he shows himself a master at it. He has written it in sextains, i.e., a quatrain followed by a couplet. This is well-suited for narrative poetry and easier to handle than the nine-line form used by Spenser in his *Faerie Queene*, which Shakespeare must have read.

The Rape of Lucrece

This is the second of his long narrative poems and resembles *Venus and Adonis* in two other matters also—it is dedicated to the Earl of Southampton and is based on Ovid. This is a much more serious poem than the former one for Shakespeare tries to analyse the feeling of guilt in Tarquin. This psychological insight raises the poem above the light-hearted narratives that were fashionable at the time. Tarquin's conflicts of emotion raise him to tragic heights. Shakespeare has given proof of his poetic craft by using the rhyme royal form.

The Sonnets

This is a sequence of a hundred and fifty-four love-sonnets, instinct with intense passion. They, as has been mentioned above (*vide* his Life, *supra*) are supposed to be autobiographical, depicting the relationship between himself and the Earl of Southampton whom he designates as Mr. W.H., "the onlie begetter" of these sonnets. The first 126 of the sonnets are addressed to him and the remaining to the equally famous Dark Lady, who was perhaps Mary Fitton, a maid of honour at Court. Usually Elizabethan love-sonnets were addressed to but one person, and Shakespeare's sequence is unique in that it explores a triangular relationship.

Titus Andronicus

This play is a Roman tragedy and also a revenge tragedy. It follows Seneca and Kyd and can be rightfully called a blood-and-thunder tragedy. It contains a well-known parody of a famous passage in Kyd's *The Spanish Tragedy*, and was extremely popular at that time.

Richard II

This play, unlike others, has a certain topical relevance. It reflects the political situation of the time so graphically that the Queen had been extremely annoyed and said, "I am Richard II, know ye that? This tragedy is played forty times in open streets and houses." The play shows the deposition of King Richard II and this was such a sensitive issue that scene had to be omitted when the play was staged.

A Midsummer Night's Dream

This is undoubtedly the best among his early comedies. It has been very popular from the beginning and continues to be so. In it, for the first time, Shakespeare introduces the supernatural element in the characters of the fairy King and Queen and their attendants. The range of characters in the play, therefore, is wider than it had formerly been, and will be equalled only by *Tempest* at the end of his career. The story goes back to the pagan times of Greece.

Love's Labour's Lost

This play has always been notable for its witty dialogues. All the characters are witty, but Lord Berowne is the wittiest of all. The characters are all from high aristocracy, there being the French King, the Princess to whom he pays court, four courtiers and four ladies. In the sub-plot humbler characters have been introduced. As has been pointed out in the life given above, the character of the happy-go-lucky, light-hearted and witty Lord Berowne is supposed to be half-autobiographical. A passage by him, renouncing flowery and ornate diction, has become famous.

King John

This play is centered round the historical figure of King John, but, indirectly, it has a life-long battle with the Church of Rome and Queen Elizabeth had done the same. This had ultimately resulted in her excommunication by the Pope. Shakespeare has always avoided religious issues and this is the only play in which he has taken it up. In spite of this, the play is not a religious one. It is actually a highly patriotic play in which foreign policy is treated as the most important theme. The character of King John has been depicted with great insight. Shakespeare shows himself well able to deal with such issues.

The Taming of the Shrew

This play was performed in 1594 and has an Italian setting. The main characters, the hero and the heroine, have been strongly and effectively sketched in. The central theme is the relationship between husband and wife, both of them aiming at supremacy over the other, an extremely popular theme of his day. It is a most entertaining and stage worthy play. Shakespeare, always mindful of neatly balancing his characters, has created another female character as foil for the shrew. This throws both the characters into relief. Shakespeare's talent for creating convincing characters can be clearly seen.

The Merchant of Venice

This is the first of his Golden Comedies. The merchant of the title should according to custom, be the hero, but it is doubtful whether he can really be called so. As a matter of fact Shylock, the villain of the piece, is such a forceful character that he towers over everyone also. One of the most important female characters, Portia, is the heroine of this play. Shakespeare makes extensive and effective use of the Elizabethan convention of disguise, for each of the three female characters don male disguises, though for a very short time. He also shows full mastery over blank verse and poetic diction in this play, using different kinds of diction for different scenes and characters.

Henry IV—Pts. I & II

These two plays are the crowning achievements of English chronicle plays. Sir John Falstaff has become the archetype of comic characters. Towards the end of the play, Prince Hal accedes to the throne as King Henry V and, leaving his days of jollity behind him, devotes himself to the duties of kingship in earnest. He has to dissociate himself from the past and therefore rejects Falstaff who had been his boon companion all these days. Though his rejection of Falstaff is fully understandable and even commendable, the cruel manner of doing it creates a lasting impression in the audience. Falstaff, however, has become immortal.

The Merry Wives of Windsor

Queen Elizabeth was so charmed by Falstaff that she ordered a play with "the fat knight in love" and Shakespeare produced this. This rollicking farce begins at the point where *Henry IV, pt. 2* ends, i.e., with Falstaff's rejection. It is a highly entertaining and stage-worthy play but has not attracted serious critical attention. One feature of the play is significant: it seems that Shakespeare had poked fun at Ben Jonson's humour characters. Corporal Nym is a parody of such a character, for he used the word "humour" in almost every sentence he speaks.

King Henry V

It has been affirmed by Shakespearean scholars that this play presents Shakespeare's concept of the ideal King. Kingship and patriotism are the twin themes of the play. Shakespeare deals with the historical battle of Agincourt in which the English won a resounding victory over the French. Shakespeare does not glorify war in a partisan manner, but, with the insight of a true poet, present the negative side of warbravery and endurance as well as death and suffering. Henry V shows himself as a strict but just King. Falstaff goes to Arthur's bosom in this play.

Much Ado About Nothing

This play is the second in the group of his four Golden Comedies. Like almost all Elizabethan comedies, it has more than one plot, and the theme is love. Shakespeare has presented the theme in two different ways. There is crude physical love which is based on appearances that prove to be deceptive. This aspect of love is presented in the Hero-Claudio plot. The Benedick-Beatrice plot takes up the theme of the rejection of married love that Shakespeare takes up repeatedly in his plays. As in the other comedies, the lovers gradually come to accept the social responsibilities of marriage though at first they are not conscious of this.

Julius Caesar

This play has been designated, along with *Coriolanus* and *Antony and Cleopatra*, as a Roman tragedy. The central theme of the play is the opposition of tyranny and liberty. It is a stern play with a stern plot which has but little of comedy in it. His characters, though historical, are all living and convincing human beings. He took the story from Lord North's translation of Plutarch's famous *Lives*. Shakespeare adopted many of the prose passages in this book into blank verse. This shows his resourcefulness. Supernatural elements are presented in the figure of Caesar's Ghost.

As You Like It

This is the happiest of his "happy" comedies, the most romantic of his romantic comedies. The main events take place in the pastoral surroundings of the forest of Arden and there are no less than four pairs of lovers, neatly married off at the end. The main theme, as in all romantic comedies, is love and it is shown here on various levels, ranging from the courtly love Rosalind-Orlando to the more earthly love of the shepherds. Disguises provide intrigue and entertainment and in Rosalind he has given a charming heroine.

Twelfth Night

This play succeeds *As You Like It*. *Twelfth Night* is the fourth and the last of the Golden Comedies. All the conventional elements of popular comedies are present in it: disguises, mistaken identities, the separation and re-union of siblings, etc. Shakespeare makes the plot even more complicated by making the separated siblings identical twins. A watered-down version of Falstaff is to be found in Sir Toby Belch, and one of the most remarkable jesters, Feste, is presented in this play. He is a highly accomplished jester, surpassed only by the unique fool in King Lear. Viola is one of the most charming heroines of our poet.

Hamlet

This is the first of the four Great Tragedies and had been, for a long time, regarded as his best. It is his longest play. It is actually a revenge tragedy, but the crudities of Kyd are left far behind and the play is so sophisticated that this feature is often overlooked. It is the unique figure of Hamlet that overshadows every element of the play. He is a far more significant figure that merely a hero with the flow of indecision.

Troilus and Cressida

This the first of the Problem Comedies and Shakespeare turns to Ancient Greece for his source material. These are all plays that deal with the most unattractive traits of human beings, presenting the seamy side of life. This particular play comes very near to a satire and gives a satirical, disillusioned treatment to the two themes of love and war.

All's Well That Ends Well

The second of the problems comedies, this play deal with the theme of the conflict between virtue and nobility. This is seen in the Bertram-Helena plot but there are several sub-themes, like the conflict between old and young generations. In this play, Shakespeare is far less tolerant of the follies and vices of humanity than he had been earlier, as the braggart soldier Parolles shows.

Macbeth

Shakespeare chose a story from Scottish history for this tragedy, thus paying a tribute to the Scottish king, James I. It is well-known as the darkest and gloomiest of his tragedies. One of the most important characters in it is that of Lady Macbeth. He has also used supernatural elements in it.

Antony and Cleopatra

This is a sequel to Julius Caesar, though it is totally different in theme. It is the theme of love that he has taken up here. The character of Cleopatra dominates the play. It is so complex that it has variously been called a history, a symphony, a political play and Roman tragedy.

Coriolanus

This is a political Roman tragedy, the last of his tragedies. Critics usually group it with the two other Roman tragedies, *Julius Caesar* and *Antony and Cleopatra*. The hero is so intrinsically noble that he is in conflict with society and therefore society rejects him. This brings about his tragic end.

Timon of Athens

Though this is a five-act problem comedy, it is generally felt that this is not a complete play. It ends with the hero's (who is a misanthrope) expulsion from society, but this is no fitting end and leaves a feeling of incompleteness in the mind of the reader.

Measure For Measure

Another problem comedy, this is a very serious play though like *As You Like It*, the merriest of the golden comedies, it ends with four marriages. The themes of justice and fidelity are the twin themes of the play. It contains one of the most charming songs of Shakespeare.

Othello

Hamlet was the last Elizabethan tragedy that Shakespeare had written, and *Othello* is the first of his Jacobean plays and the second of the four Great Tragedies. It has been called the *Romeo and Juliet* of his later phase and treats the theme of jealousy. One of his most important villains, Iago, comes in this play about whom the famous phrase "motiveless malignity" had been used by Coleridge.

King Lear

This is the play regarded at present as the greatest of his tragedies. It depicts, not merely the follies of King Lear and his tragic fate, but the predicaments of man himself in a cruel universe. The play has, therefore, been called a cosmic drama. A primitive legend has been transformed into a terrible tragedy that has the qualities of sublimity and universality in it. One of the unique characters in it is that of the Fool who serves many complex purposes. Dante's *Divine Comedy* is one of the works with which this play has been compared.

Pericles, Cymbeline, The Winter's Tale and The Tempest

This group is known as the last Romances and the same theme, repeatedly, occurs in them. This is the theme of sin, repentance and forgiveness. Alongside this, runs the theme of a tainted and chastened older generation. *The Tempest* is his last play, acted to celebrate a royal betrothal. Shakespeare had acted in the role of Prospero and blessed the royal couple. Prospero's renunciation is thought to be Shakespeare's farewell to the theatre.

Henry VIII

Modern scholars agree in attributing this play to Shakespeare, though this had been a matter of controversy for a long time. It takes up the theme of patience in adversity. Not only does the King himself learn patience but so do the other characters as well. It ends with an affirmation of the continuity of life.

The Two Noble Kinsmen

This is a work of collaboration with Fletcher. Shakespeare wrote the major parts of Act I and also part of Acts III and V. Many of his contemporaries had collaborated with others, but this is the only such work of Shakespeare. When Fletcher introduced a rather vulgar sub-plot, Shakespeare left off working with him. The story is taken from Chaucer.

References

1. The dates for these works have been taken from *The New Caxton Encyclopaedia*, London, Caxton Pubs. Ltd., 1982. 20 vols.
2. Cited in Halliday, F.E., *The Life of Shakespeare*. London, Gerald Duckworth & Co. Ltd., 1961, p. 20.
3. *As You Like It*, Act II, scene vii, 11.145-147, p. 38. Ware, Wordsworth Classics, 1993.
4. Ribner, Irving, *William Shakespeare; Life, Times and Theatre*, London, John Wiley and Sons Inc., 1969, pp. 38-39.
5. Craig, H., *op.cit.*, p. 52. Citation.
6. Halliday, F.E., *op.cit.*, p. 60.

7. Quoted in Ribner, I., *op.cit.*, p. 45.
8. Quoted in Rowse, A.L., *William Shakespeare: A biography*, London, Macmillan & Co. Ltd., 1963, p. 100.
9. Quoted in Halliday, *op.cit.*, pp. 102-03.
10. Rowse, A.L., *op.cit.*, p. 201.
11. Halliday, *op.cit.*, p. 118.
12. *Ibid.*, p. 138, Ribner, *op.cit.*, p. 52 and many others.
13. Spencer, Theodore, *Shakespeare and the Nature of Man*. New York, the Macmillan Company, 1945, p. 49.
14. Quoted in Ribner, *op.cit.*, p. 64, and by many others.
15. Fluchère, H., *Shakespeare*, London, Longman & Green, 1953, p. 54.
16. *Ibid.*, p. 265.

4

The Story and the Genre

(a) A Brief Outline

The story of *Othello* is essentially a tragic story of love and is quite simple. There are no subplots in it and though there are many intrigues, these never attain the depth or expanse to be called subplots. *Othello*, from this point of view is an uncommon play, for usually these play have more than one plot.

As A.C. Bradley has pointed out, the story is almost contemporaneous with Shakespeare, for the attack on Cyprus by the Turks which takes Othello to that island took place in 1570 (*vide* Chapter 9 *infra*). Othello the hero, is a Moor in the service of Venice, as is made clear in the list of the *Dramatis Personae*. He is a noble warrior and an eloquent speaker. This eloquence has won him the love of Desdemona, the daughter of Brabantio who is a senator. Knowing that Brabantio will never consent to marry his daughter to a Moor, the lovers decide to run away to marry. This news is given to Brabantio by Iago and Roderigo, the villain and the fool respectively. But, even as he is searching for the truants, news comes to the Senate that the Turks are going to attack Cyprus. The Senate, instead of punishing Othello as Brabantio had expected, appoints him the commander and sends him to Cyprus to save the island. The rest of the play takes place in Cyprus. Desdemona accompanies him.

Iago, Desdemona, Emilia and Roderigo come to Cyprus before Othello does. They are preceded by Cassio, a noble Venetian and Othello's lieutenant. There is a terrible storm which drown the Turkish fleet, so Othello is at liberty to devote himself to Desdemona.

Both Iago and Roderigo have a grudge against Othello. Iago hates him as Othello has deprived him of promotion and appointed Cassio, a lieutenant over his head. Roderigo dislikes him as he himself was a suitor for Desdemona and Othello marries her. Iago makes a fool of him by telling him that sooner or later Desdemona will get tired of Othello and then his time will come. Misled by these assurances, Roderigo comes to Cyprus. Iago also believes that Cassio is in love with Desdemona and he plans to make Othello jealous of him. Thus we see the beginnings of intrigues in Iago's mind. Knowing full well that Desdemona is loyal and loves only Othello, he yet thinks of telling him that Cassio and she are having an adulterous love-affair. He also believes that Othello has had an affair with his own wife Emilia, and this has made him loathe Othello even more. As he hates Cassio for having superseded him, his devilish plan will ruin him also.

He plans first of all to set Othello against Cassio, for Othello likes Cassio very much. He knows that Cassio gets drunk very easily and once drunk he becomes extremely quarrelsome. So he calls party of young men together and plies him with wine and makes him drunk. Cassio then attacks Roderigo and then Montano. He wounds the latter. Montano is an important person for he was the previous governor of Cyprus, prior to Othello. Iago sends Roderigo to rouse the neighbourhood with the news that mutiny has broken out in the garrison. Soon an alarm bell rings which brings Othello to the spot. He is justifiably angry and punishes Cassio by demoting him.

By this time, Cassio has recovered his senses and has realised that he has ruined himself. Iago tells him not to despair and advises him to meet Desdemona and ask her, to plead for him. He agrees to this. Iago thus moves in a very well-planned manner for if it succeeds then Desdemona will plead for Cassio and it will be possible for Iago to hint at an illicit relationship between them. He decides that, first of all, he will tell Emilia, his wife, to plead for Cassio to Desdemona even before he approaches her. This is what he calls a "double knavery".

Then he begins to plant the seeds of jealousy in Othello's heart. He does it very cleverly, with hints and insinuations. Desdemona comes to Othello and pleads for Cassio in all innocence and Othello too, with a mind completely free at first, of jealousy or suspicion, agrees to take Cassio back. There is an all-encompassing love for Desdemona in Othello, as he makes clear in one of the most effective passages in the play:

> Excellent wretch ! perdition catch my soul
> But I do love thee, and when I love thee not
> Chaos is come again.[1]

Iago's insinuations begin after this speech. He pretends to be most unwilling to tell Othello anything but contrives to make him highly suspicious. Finally he tells him to observe his wife when she is with Cassio. It is noticeable that he is the one to first use the word "jealousy" and Othello:

> O beware jealousy;
> It is the green-ey'd monster which doth mock
> That meat it feeds on.[2]

After this there is no peace for Othello. He thinks of two reasons why Desdemona could have ceased to love him—that he is black, and that he is too old for her.

While he is still thinking of all this, Desdemona and Emilia come to call him for dinner and on going out Desdemona drops her handkerchief. It is the first gift that Othello had given her, and Iago had asked Emilia to steal it and give it to him many times. Now she takes the chance to pick it up and, even while she is saying how Iago had asked her to steal it, he himself comes.

She gives the handkerchief to him and hardly has she left the stage when Othello arrives, and demands proof of Desdemona's infidelity. Iago makes use of the opportunity and tells him that Cassio has got the handkerchief for Desdemona has given it him as a love-token. On hearing this, Othello kneels down and takes a solemn vow to be revenged on Cassio and Desdemona. Iago, to show his loyalty, also vows to help him. This moves Othello so much that, then and there, he appoints Iago his lieutenant. Thus at one stroke, Iago's aim, which he himself had called "double knavery" is achieved. He has ruined Cassio and taken his place and he has also destroyed the peace of Othello's mind forever.

Othello demands to see the handkerchief and Desdemona naturally cannot show it to him. This does but confirm Othello's belief in her infidelity. Now Iago had planted the handkerchief in Cassio's lodgings, and he, finding it, gives it to Bianca, his mistress. Thus every coincidence favours Iago. By this time, Othello is in such a state of intense jealousy that he who used to be an eloquent speaker can hardly speak coherently and falls down in a faint.

When Othello recovers, Iago tells him to withdraw so that he can eavesdrop on the conversation between himself and Cassio. When Cassio comes in a few moments later, he in a low voice mentions Bianca to him. This makes Cassio laugh and Othello sees this. He naturally assumes that they are talking of Desdemona. While this is going on, again fate favours Iago and Bianca herself comes in, with Desdemona's handkerchief in her hand. Othello recognizes it.

After they have both gone, Othello and Iago try to think of a way to kill Desdemona and Iago tells him to strangle her in the bed she has polluted. The rough justice of this appeals to Othello. Meanwhile an embassy comes from Venice. Lodovico has come with a letter from the Senate which recalls Othello to Venice, appointing Cassio as the governor of Cyprus in his stead. It is in this scene, at this time, and in front of everyone, that Othello insults Desdemona.

He later questions Emilia about Desdemona's possible infidelity and Emilia tells him that she is fully loyal to him. When Desdemona comes in Othello talks to her as if she were a strumpet in a brothel.

After this Iago manages things in such a way that both Roderigo and Cassio are wounded. He has promised Othello that he would punish Cassio and he keeps his word. Actually he had promised to kill Cassio, but he cannot manage this.

By this time we have reached the end of the play. Desdemona is asleep, Othello comes in and waking her, questions her about her deceitfulness. She denies his charges, but this makes him all the more angry. Then he kills her. After this Emilia comes in, bringing the news of the fight between Roderigo and Cassio, and discovers Desdemona's murder. Now she also tells him about the handkerchief—how Desdemona had dropped it and she had picked it up and given it to Iago. At her cries for help, the others come in and the position is clarified by Othello and Emilia. Othello of course, realises the enormity of what he had done, and Iago's villainy is fully exposed. Iago then kills Emilia and tries to escape. He is caught, however, and awaits punishment. Othello punishes himself by committing suicide. Thus the tragic doom enveloping the main characters is fulfilled. Cassio is entrusted with the task of restoring order and maintaining peace at Cyprus. The tragedy, however, concerns only the hero and the heroine and their immediate associates.

(b) The Genre of the Play

It would seem that the classification of *Othello* would be a simple and straightforward matter—it is a domestic tragedy, like *Romeo and Juliet*. It has, indeed been called the *Romeo and Juliet* of his later phase. Yet here too, as over the other aspects of the play, many opinions have been given by Shakespearean critics. We shall now have a look at some of these views.

(i) *A Domestic Tragedy*

This is the most widely held view of the play as far as its genre is concerned. The tragedy at that time, as has been mentioned in the *Introduction*, was divided into four categories: (a) Revenge tragedy, (b) Conqueror tragedy, (c) Villain tragedy and (d) Domestic tragedy. Othello, it is commonly thought, belongs to the last category. The death of the hero and the heroine does not affect a whole kingdom in this kind of tragedy, but only a family and therefore the epithet "domestic" is attached to it. *Arden of Feversham* and *A Yorkshire Tragedy* (ascribed to Shakespeare earlier) are two more examples of such plays. As far as Othello is concerned, it can be seen from the summary given above that only the family and the immediate associates of *Othello* are affected. In fact the family ceases to exist as only the two of them make up the family. There are certain other elements in the play, for example, in the very first scene Iago brings up the motif of revenge and later Othello says that he will be revenged on Cassio. Yet the play can never be called a revenge tragedy. Throughout the play, we are made aware of the domestic environment. Referring to the famous willow-song in particular, G. Wilson Knight says:

> The extreme beauty and pathos of this scene are largely dependent on the domesticity of it. Othello is eminently a domestic tragedy.[3]

The majority of the critics agree with this view. We do not have the impression, as with *Macbeth* and the other tragedies, of misfortune overtaking an entire kingdom. Only one family is concerned, and that a minuscule one, as it consists of only two members. It can be widened to include Brabantio, Desdemona's father, who also dies of a broken heart, as Desdemona has left home. Emilia is not related to either Othello or Desdemona, but she is the latter's constant companion. The only person to die who is entirely unrelated to either of them is Roderigo. He did not really have to die, but Shakespeare thought it best.

(ii) *Tragedy of Mind*

John Bayley finds Othello to be a hero who lives in his mind. This would seem to be paradoxical because Othello is eminently a man of action, a successful and valiant general. Yet according to this critic, he is a man who is regulated primarily by his mind. Pointing out the difference between different kinds of men, he says:

> Some could have done Macbeth's deeds and not lost a wink of sleep for it. The tragedies of mind bring out the difference graphically and inevitably and distinguishes those who live in the mind. Othello is the most unexpected hero to do so.[4]

He then proceeds to analyse the play from this point of view. He shows how Othello dwells on his feelings and emotions. Though, he is a man of action, his mental condition is of extreme importance to the dramatist as well as to himself. His faith in Desdemona makes up his whole world and he allows himself to be deluded in this. So, for him, "chaos is come again". His world is destroyed. He is an idealist so far as love is concerned, in direct opposition to Iago. In his mind, love is different from sex and this "polarisation" renders Othello incapable of reacting otherwise than he does. The first two Acts make us look upon Othello as a valiant and idealistic man of action and a man of honour with it. So we would expect that he would not believe Iago's insinuations, but, contrary to our expectations he does believe in them. In this, Othello is different from Hamlet and also from Macbeth. John Bayley, in other words is accusing Shakespeare of having created an inconsistent character, and consistency is one of the most important features of dramatic characters as given by Aristotle (*vide* Chapter 7 *infra* for more information).

Apart from this feature, this critic repeatedly points out the difference between Othello, and Hamlet and Macbeth. He shows how the two latter also ratiocinate about the murder they are about to commit. He brings in many other factors and points out that Othello's pre-occupation with his own mind rather than with external events alienates the reader's or the audience's sympathy from him. Othello's attitude to love, his uncontrollable jealousy, his propensity for being gulled, all bring the play very close to comedy, and he finds Rymer's phrase "bloody farce" to be of special significance as it combines the elements of tragedy and comedy. All this is possible because it is play in which it is the mind of Othello that dominates the entire play.

(iii) *A Tragedy of Privacy*

After having discussed Othello as a tragedy of the mind, Bayley asserts that it is a tragedy of privacy. He analyses the character of Desdemona and it is from her point of view that he calls the play a "tragedy of privacy". Desdemona is primarily a wife and she looks upon Othello from that, an entirely domestic, point of view. He is her husband and she, like a good wife, has to look after him, seeing to it that he puts on his gloves to keep warm and eats good wholesome food. These wifely concerns are of the greatest importance to her. They are an inalienable part of married life, a part of her own life. She looks upon such duties as the unquestioned, automatic part of her life-automatic, but nonetheless of paramount importance in marital life:

> 'Tis as I should entreat you wear your gloves,
> Or feed on nourishing dishes, or keep you warm.[5]

In their domestic life, he is first of all her husband and his importance as a soldier, as a hero, as a general are side-issues:

> In his wife's eye and mind...Othello is none of the things spectators have found him, neither heroic nor credulous, no monster and not a god either, but a man capable alike of good and bad.[6]

It is the private domestic life of a married couple that is of importance to Desdemona and this is the reason why it is "tragedy of privacy". This critic is aware of the fact that this phrase is itself incongruous, for according to him Shakespeare has chosen to treat his subject in a manner unsuited to the form of a tragedy. Even so, the label "tragedy of privacy" can be justifiably applied to this play. It is slightly different from the term "domestic tragedy", which is somewhat wider in its implications. "Domestic tragedy" can include an entire family and its immediate associates. Bayley's term, however, is much narrower in its implications, for he seems to mean only a married couple. In that case, it will be difficult to explain the significance of the death of Emilia, far less that of Roderigo. Brabantio's death, too, will fall outside the periphery. Bayley's phrase restricts and imposes limits to Shakespeare, but the very fact that the same critic can find two different terms in the same essay, "tragedy of mind", and "tragedy of privacy", to explain the nature of the play shows how complex the play itself is.

(iv) *Tragedy of Misunderstanding*

This is how John Wain categorises *Othello*. He is of the opinion that the characters all misunderstand each other; they are always at cross purposes. Not only this: they do not understand their own selves at all clearly. Othello does not understand Desdemona at all. If he did he would know that she is not the kind of wife who would betray him. Her attitude to marital infidelity is made clear in the willow-scene when she says:

> Beshrew me, if I would do such a wrong,
> For the whole world.
>
> ... ...
>
> I do not think there is any such woman.[7]

Nor does Desdemona understand Othello's attitude to her properly. He does not look upon her as a wife, but as a divinity, as magnificent creature who has glorified him by loving him. Therefore, the least breath of suspicion about her chastity would drive him nearly mad. This is a basically Petrarchan attitude. He almost echoes Desdemona's lines quoted above when he asserts that he would not give her up for the whole world:

> If heaven would make me such another world,
> Of one entire and perfect chrysolite,
> I'd not have sold her for it.[8]

The two of them are of the same mind, but they do not understand each other.

Likewise, this critic examines the relationship between each of the characters and points out how they all have a false opinion of each other and how they do not have a proper knowledge of their own selves either. This extends even to Iago. He does not know that he is at bottom a sadist. Nor does he know the power of the kind of love that has overmastered Othello. He, thus, cannot imagine the kind of suffering he is inflicting on Othello, nor can he visualise the terrible end that plunges all of them into the abyss of death, annihilating all of them. *Othello*, thus, basically, is tragedy of misunderstanding:

> No one among the characters understands anyone else; nor are they, for the most part, very strong on self-understanding either.[9]

He analyses the situation of each character and explains how the misunderstandings have become possible. Desdemona has led a very protected life and does not know anything about men. Othello, from boyhood, has been a soldier, and does not know anything about sophisticated upper class Venetian society.

Like this, with each case, misunderstandings have become possible.

(v) *A Drama of Modern Life*

This is the view held by A.C. Bradley. He points out that the date of the Turkish attack on Cyprus was 1570, so the play at the time of its first performance was a story of almost contemporary life. *Othello* more than any other of the four great tragedies refers to our life and the individuals of our own age. One cannot regard the events of *Hamlet* or *Macbeth*, least of all of *King Lear* as being relevant to our own age, but *Othello* is contemporaneous with us. As a character also, the hero has more of individual appeal for us than the other tragic heroes. The intense emotions experienced by him have reference to men of all time and the events that take place in the play can take place in the modern age as well. This factor actually means that the characters in *Othello* are fully universalised, but this is not the way that Bradley chooses to look at the play. He first of all highlights the fact that it is a domestic tragedy, which means that it is more a story of the life of a private individual than the other tragedies of Shakespeare. The next step of the argument leads to the assertion that whatever happens in the play can happen equally easily today, more easily than the events of the other tragedies:

> *Othello* is a drama of modern life.... The characters come close to us, and the application of the drama to ourselves (if the phrase may be pardoned) is more immediate than it can be in *Hamlet* or in *King Lear*.[10]

These are some of the most prominent classifications of the play. Besides these, there are many more. *Othello* has, for example, been called a Christian tragedy in which Othello's downfall has been compared with that of Adam and what happens to Desdemona is the inversion of that which happens to Eve. It has also been called a diagram or allegorical representation of Spanish political history in which the hero represents Philip II and Iago his enemy Antonio Perez.[11] Such diversity of critical opinions on the relatively simple subject of the genre of the play serves to highlight its complexity.

References

1. *Othello*, Act III, sc. ii, lines 91-93, p. 98. All the quotations are taken from the Arden edition, edited by Ridley, M.R., London, Methuen, University Paperback, 1984 report. Quotations from the text as well as the remarks from Ridley will be from this edition, unless indicated otherwise.
2. Act III, sc. iii. ll. 169-71, p. 103.
3. Knight, G. Wilson, *The Wheel of Fire*, London, Methuen & Co. Ltd., 1977, p. 108.
4. Bayley, John, *Tragedy and Consciousness: Othello*, in Wain, John, *op.cit.*, p. 154.
5. Act III, sc. iii, ll. 178-79, p. 97.
6. Bayley, John, *op.cit.*, p. 176.
7. Act IV, sc. iii, ll. 77-78, 83, pp. 167-68.
8. Act V, sc. ii, ll. 145-47, p. 185.
9. Wain, John, *op.cit.*, p. 12.
10. Bradley, A.C., *Shakespearean Tragedy*, London, Macmillan & Co. Ltd., 1960 rpt., p. 346.
11. Wain, John, *op.cit.*, p. 16.

5

A Scene-wise Analysis

Act I, scene i

The play is opened by Iago the villain and Roderigo the fool. It is made clear by Roderigo that he has a grudge against Iago who has taken a large amount of money from him on some pretext. Later it becomes clear that Roderigo is one of the suitors of Desdemona and Iago has taken money from him in order to further his suit with her, all the time knowing that she is in love with Othello and the two of them mean to marry. He did not tell Roderigo anything about this, so his duplicity is clear even from the first lines.

Iago then tells Roderigo that he hates Othello because he has appointed Cassio his lieutenant over Iago's head. Then he tells the young man to shout and rouse Brabantio, Desdemona's father and tell him that his daughter has run away. He thinks that Brabantio, who is a prominent citizen and a senator, must do something to poison Othello's triumph. They then shout, which wakens Brabantio.

He has no idea that Desdemona is not in her room. It is here that it becomes clear that Roderigo is the rejected suitor of Desdemona. Brabantio had rejected him:

> I have charg'd thee not to haunt about my doors;
> In honest plainness thou hast heard me say
> My daughter is not for thee.[1]

Brabantio finds that Desdemona is really not in her room and becomes alarmed and angry. Roderigo assures him that Othello and she have got married. Brabantio decides to call up his relatives and neighbours to support him and get Desdemona back by saying that Othello has used witchcraft in luring her away.

The scene ends here. Elizabethan plays were usually written in a mixture of prose and verse. Aristocratic characters speak in verse and humble ones in prose. This scene is a mixture of the two. There are two passages spoken by Iago which are in prose. Iago has many passages in prose in the play. Usually he speaks in a coarse manner in the prose passages, as he does here. As a matter of fact, the rule about prose and verse was not an inflexible one Noble characters, on occasion, could speak in prose, and humble ones in verse.

None of Shakespeare's scene is dispensable, and each scene is interlinked with the previous and the following ones. As we read each scene, this and other features shall be pointed out. Since the present scene is the very first, it cannot be linked to any previous one, but it is definitely linked to the ensuing ones. It prepares us for the next scene by telling us of the marriage of Othello and Desdemona. That is the function of all opening scenes—they are linked in various ways to the ensuring ones. Iago's attitude to Othello prepares us for his villainy. The matter of the latter's marriage, which is only mentioned here, will be dealt with in detail in the next scene.

Most of Shakespeare's scenes, particularly if they are long ones, fall into certain divisions. This scene, too, can be divided into two clear cut sections. The first section consists of the dialogue between Iago and Roderigo up till line 81. Then from Brabantio's appearance at a window, the second section starts and continues till the end. The first section is slightly shorter than the second as it consists of 81 lines and the whole scene is of 184 lines. This often happens. Sometimes the different sections are well-balanced, sometimes not.

The scene is a highly functional one in that it also introduces one major character, Iago, and two minor ones, Roderigo and Brabantio. Apart from this, it acts as the Prologue (*vide* Chapter 9, *infra*, for more information on this head) to the play. As such it introduces the main theme of the play, the love between Othello and Desdemona and also destruction in the hatred of Iago. The hero and the heroine are not presented in person, but preparations are made for their appearance. Othello, it is true, is not named, but there are many comments on his personality.

Desdemona is not only named, but we also come to know her family background, that she is a girl much sought after, and that she is beautiful.

A special feature of the opening scene has been pointed out by M.R. Ridley. According to him this scene paints, through Iago, a thoroughly misleading picture of Othello which colour our perception of his character:

> The picture which we get…is surely that of an efficient, perhaps even great, but blustering and erratic, soldier of fortune, of no morals and unsound judgments.[2]

This picture gets corrected later on. We perceive him to be a dignified and laconic man, with no bluster about him. This is an unusual procedure for Shakespeare—to give a different impression of the hero before bringing him on the stage, from that which is given later on. Ridley is of the opinion that Shakespeare has done this deliberately for three reasons:

(1) He makes us distrust Iago.
(2) He is, from the outset, creating suspense.
(3) We are forced, when "he" does enter to make our own picture of "him".[3]

The first scene thus is an extremely significant one, as is the case with all of Shakespeare's plays.

Act I, scene ii

In point of time this scene takes place just a little after the preceding one. Othello and Iago are talking and Othello makes clear that he knows his own worth. It is a dignified speech but Anthony Hecht thinks differently:

> Meant to be immediately recognized as ludicrous and nervous vanity.[4]

After just thirty-three lines of dialogue the Duke's men enter with torches, accompanied by Cassio, who has brought Othello an urgent summons from the Duke. It seems that some business of moment has happened at Cyprus. Several messages have come to the Duke from there. He, in his turn, has sent for the consuls and for Othello. After a few more lines of dialogue, Brabantio enters with Roderigo and his own armed men. They are ready to fight but Othello stops them with a line that has become famous as one of the most effective lines:

> Keep up your bright swords, for the dew will rust them.[5]

Brabantio accuses him of having used witchcraft in making Desdemona fall in love with him. Othello, with great dignity, asks what he should do and Brabantio tells him that he should be in prison till his trial. But this is not possible for, as Othello tells him, the Duke is in council and has sent him urgent summons. Though it is night, the Duke has called an urgent meeting. So everyone gets ready to go to the Senate House and the scene comes to an end.

This scene is entirely in verse and is also a very short one, containing only ninety-nine lines. There is one feature to be noted about the blank verse used in this scene. The scene ends with Brabantio's speech which ends with a couplet:

> For if such actions may have passage free,
> Bond-slaves, and pagans, shall our statesmen be.[6]

This is called a Senecan couplet. Seneca used such couplets to point out a móral and as the Elizabethans were deeply influenced by him they too used such couplets in their plays. It is quite well-known a feature of their poetry that their blank verse is often broken up by such couplets. This couplet is the first such in this play.

The scene is directly linked to the foregoing and the ensuing ones as it carries forward the action that had been started in the preceding scene. In that scene Brabantio had been told of the elopement and possible marriage of Othello and Desdemona and here we have the enraged father coming and hurling accusations at Othello.

Its looks forward to the next scene in that here the Duke's emergency meeting under way. Thus the scene prepares us for the next.

Though it is a short scene yet it falls into three clear divisions. The first part comprises thirty-three lines and lasts till the entrance of Cassio bringing the Duke's summons. The second part is even shorter, comprising only twenty-one lines and carries on till line 54, till the entrance of Brabantio. The next part begins with the entrance of Brabantio and continues till the end of the scene, for forty-five lines. In it we have the attempt to take Othello as prisoner which fails as he is needed by the Duke. Shakespeare thus provides variety and action even in this short scene. It is a very stage-worthy scene, beginning quietly with the dialogue between Othello and Iago, then speeding up with the entrance of Cassio. More characters and action are introduced when Brabantio enters. The scene is important in that it introduces the hero, for whom an entirely negative preparation had been made in the former scene (*vide* the opinion of Ridley given above). It also introduces Cassio, the unwitting cause of tragedy. From this point of view, though short, it is an important scene. Several points are made clear to the audience: Othello's marriage to Desdemona, some important event at Cyprus, Othello's importance to the Duke. These points are taken up in the next scene.

Act I, scene iii

This is the second longest scene in the play. It takes place in the council chambers of Venice. In the foregoing scene, we had been told that the Duke has called a meeting at which he requires the presence of Othello, and in this scene we have that meeting.

The senators have each been sent letters from Cyprus, apprising them of an attempt by a Turkish fleet to invade them. While the senators are still talking, two more messages come. The latest message is that the Turkish fleet has joined up with another fleet at Rhodes and now the entire fleet is making for Cyprus. While the senators are discussing this development, Othello and Brabantio enter. Before the Duke can explain to Othello why he has been summoned, Brabantio starts accusing him. He says that Othello had used witchcraft to make Desdemona fall in love with him. The Duke then asks Othello what he has to say to this and the latter, in a highly dignified speech says that it is true that he has married Desdemona and he is ready to disclose what withcraft he had used. They send for Desdemona to come to bear witness and meanwhile, in a famous speech, Othello tells the senate how he used to visit Brabantio and tell him of the many exploits and adventures that he had undergone in his life. It captivated Desdemona. She became attracted to him:

> She lov'd me for the danger I had pass'd,
> And I loved her that she did pity them.
> This is the only witchcraft I have us'd.[7]

Hearing this, the Duke says "I think this tale would win my daughter too" and we realize that he favours Othello. Thus Othello's battle here is already won because the other senators will follow him. Besides, the Duke needs Othello.

When Desdemona comes, Brabantio asks her whom she is going to obey, her father or her husband and she says, most politely, that as she is married her first obedience should go to her husband. Brabantio at once gives up his claim. Both the Duke and Brabantio then deliver two moralising speeches.

The Duke then turns to Othello and tells him of the impending attack on Cyprus. He gives the generalship of the army to Othello to repel the attack. This means that he will have to leave for Cyprus at once. Desdemona herself decides to go with him since neither Brabantio nor she likes the idea of her staying at her former home. Othello then gives Iago the charge of bringing her to Cyprus, with his own wife Emilia, to look after her. It is here that the term "honest" is applied to him and will be applied repeatedly, by himself as well as others (*vide* Chapter 7, *infra*).

Before he leaves, Brabantio makes a highly suggestive remark to Othello about Desdemona:

> Look to her, Moor, have a quick eye to see:
> She has deceived her father, may do thee.[8]

This remark, at present unheeded, will work its poison later. Just at present Othello returns, in half a line: "My life upon her faith". As will be seen, he will give his life, but after taking hers.

Then everyone goes out, leaving Roderigo and Iago on the stage. Roderigo is in a desperate frame of mind but Iago encourages him. He tells Roderigo that, soon enough, Desdemona will tire of Othello and be ready for a lover. That will be the time for Roderigo to pitch in. He advises Roderigo to take a considerable amount of money and be ready for any event. He must take heart and follow them to Cyprus.

Then Iago is left alone on the stage and we have the first of his eight soliloquies (*vide* Chapter 9, *Certain Elizabethan Features*, for more information on this head). There are two characters in this play who speak soliloquies: Othello and Iago. Of these two, Iago has eight soliloquies whereas Othello has only three of them. In this first soliloquy, we come to know his motives and his plot. He clearly says he hates Othello, for he suspects him of having committed adultery with his wife. He is furious with Cassio for having superseded him and with Othello for having made this supersession possible. So in this soliloquy he is planning "a double knavery". He will poison Othello's mind with the suggestion that Cassio is having an adulterous affair with Desdemona. Thus in this soliloquy he forms his plan of revenge;

> In this, his first soliloquy, he is concentrating primarily upon supplanting Cassio; revenge on Othello is so far only secondary.[9]

Iago ends the scene and his soliloquy with a Senecan couplet, summing up his plans:

> I ha't, it is engender'd; Hell and night
> Must bring this monstrous birth to the world's light.[10]

Quite a considerable part of this scene is in prose. The entire dialogue between Iago and Roderigo (eighty lines) is in prose and so is a short speech (eight lines) by the Duke. Then there are many Senecan couplets also, for the Duke's moral speech is entirely in them, comprising nine couplets. After this there is a speech by Brabantio in the same meter, containing five couplets. Then there is another by Brabantio, cautioning Othello against Desdemona's supposed deceitfulness. At the end, we have another by Iago. Thus, as far as versification is concerned, the scene offers unusual variety.

The scene is firmly linked to the preceding one in that it continues the two main concerns of the former: Othello's marriage and the attack on Cyprus, and both of them come to a head in this scene. The matter of Othello's marriage is satisfactorily concluded and that of Cyprus begun. It is also linked to the first scene in further clarification of Iago's motives for revenge and his plans for its execution. It is linked to the next scene in that in the next scene we have the arrival of the main characters in Cyprus, which is arranged in this one.

It is a very long scene, containing four hundred and two lines. In this it is second only to the third scene of Act three and can be divided into four parts. The first part lasts till the entrance of Brabantio, Othello and the others after line 47. The second part last till Brabantio's Senecan couplets (l. 220). The third part begins with the Duke's prose speech and lasts till the exit of Othello and Desdemona (l. 300). The last part consists of the dialogue between Iago and Roderigo and Iago's soliloquy. It can also be said that Iago's soliloquy constitutes a part by itself. In that case the scene will fall into five parts, with Iago's soliloquy making up the last. The second of these, containing Othello's speeches of self-defence is the longest.

It is an important scene as it introduces Desdemona. Preparations had been made for her entrance in the earlier scenes. We had been told that she is a sought after girl, as Roderigo is one of her suitors. Brabantio also had described her as demure and obedient girl.

It is important from another point of view in that it shows the deviousness and machiavellianism of Iago, thus foreshadowing later events. The first soliloquy, as given here, is extremely revealing. It shows Iago giving several motives for his plans to ruin Cassio and Othello at the same time. This is what has led Coleridge to make his famous remark:

> The last speech [Iago's soliloquy,] the motive-hunting of motive-less malignity—how awful! In itself fiendish.[11]

The scene is important from another point of view because it concludes the first Act. Usually, in the first Act all the main characters are introduced and Shakespeare has done this. Only a few minor characters still remain to be brought in. The action is begun in the first Act and that requirement is also fulfilled for we have the marriage of Othello, and Iago's devilish plan is formed in this scene. Of the minor characters, Emilia is the most important, and she has already been mentioned as the one to look after and accompany Desdemona. As a first Act it is successful also in that it creates in our mind the suspense necessary for drama. We look forward to the next scene in order to find out how far Iago's plans succeed.

Act II, scene i

The locale of the play changes with this scene. The rest of the play will take place in Cyprus, where this scene is situated. This is a crucial scene, as it is with this that the main action of the play starts. Indeed, G. Wilson Knight has remarked:

> This scene is a microcosm of the play, reflecting its actions.[12]

The scene is opened by Montano who used to be the governor of Cyprus till Othello's appointment, and two gentlemen. They have come to the sea-side to see the state of the weather. There has been a terrible storm and they hope that it has destroyed the Turkish fleet. Then Cassio enters and while he is expressing the hope that Othello's ship has not been harmed by the tempest they hear that the ship carrying Desdemona, Iago, Emilia and Roderigo has come to port. These four then enter the stage. There is some light-hearted badinage and then, just to entertain Desdemona, Iago starts reciting an impromptu doggerel about different kinds of women. There are ten couplets in all, broken up into separate units by prose dialogues in between. This passage has been adversely criticised by Rymer and praised by Granville-Barker. Thus Rymer stigmatises it for being vulgar and below the notice of Desdemona:

> Now follows a long rabble of Jack pudding farce between Iago and Desdemona, that runs on with all the little plays, jingle, and tyrash below the patience of any Country Kitchenmaid.[13]

Granville-Barker, on the other hand analyses the passage and praises it for creating dramatic suspense in a masterly manner:

> Shakespeare now, stimulates suspense by giving no less than a ninety-line stretch of the scene to showing us

> Desdemona's silent anxiety which he frames (for emphasis by contrast) in a bout of artificially comic distraction.[14]

Apart from the fact that one does not like to criticise Shakespeare for being vulgar, it can be seen that Granville-Barker's opinion is being supported by Desdemona herself:

> I am not merry, but I do beguile
> The thing I am, by seeming otherwise.[15]

Then, after a poisonous aside by Iago, Othello comes. They greet each other ecstatically. Then all but Iago and Roderigo leave the stage.

Now a dialogue follows between the two. Iago convinces Roderigo that Desdemona is in love with Cassio. He tells Roderigo to pick a quarrel with Cassio, inducing him to fight so that he will be suspended from service. When Cassio goes away, Iago assures Roderigo, Desdemona will fall in love with him. Then Roderigo goes away and we have the second soliloquy of Iago. He is quite sure that Cassio is in love with Desdemona and this, to his mind, means that Desdemona is also in love with Cassio. Once more he talks about his suspicions that Emilia has betrayed him with Othello and says he thirsts for revenge. He decides that he will get even with both Cassio and Othello by making Othello jealous of Cassio and grateful to him for having opened his eyes. His plan is almost ready, only the details have to be worked out. This he confesses in the last couplet that ends, his soliloquy as well as the scene:

> 'tis here, but yet confus'd;
> Knavery's plain face is never seen, till us'd.[16]

This scene, like, the previous one, is in a mixture of prose and verse. The entire dialogue between Iago and Roderigo is in prose, besides which there are several prose passages in the dialogue between Iago and Desdemona. There is variety in versification also, for there are the couplet passages by Iago which come to a total of ten couplets. Then right at the end there is the Senecan couplet quoted above. Thus the poet has provided variety in the medium he has used, just as he had done in the foregoing scene.

The scene is linked to the preceding one. In that scene, there was the discussion on the Turkish attack and the mention of all these characters going to Cyprus. This scene continues the same action. It also looks forward to the third scene because in this one, Iago plots the downfall of Cassio and in the third scene he achieves his aim. It also shows the intensity of love between Othello and Desdemona. It was necessary to show this, for this is the central theme of the play. Only by showing the depth of Othello's love for Desdemona can his later action and mood be understood, if not explained. Othello, on seeing her safely arrived at Cyprus, is ecstatic;

> O my soul's joy,
> If after every tempest come such calmness,
> May the winds blow, till they have waken'd death.
> ... ...
> If it were now to die,
> 'Twere now to be most happy, for I fear
> My soul hath her content so absolute,
> That not another comfort, like to this
> Succeeds in unknown fate.[17]

Such lines may seem to be extravagant, but in his case they state the exact truth.

This scene, like the preceding one, is quite long, comprising 307 lines and falls into three divisions. The first of these consists of the dialogue between Montano and the Gentlemen and lasts till the entrance of Cassio (l. 42). The second section, starting from line no. 43 with the entrance of Cassio, covers the entrance of all the main characters and lasts till l. 212 when all of them go out, except for Iago and Roderigo. The third section covers the rest of the scene, from line nos. 213 to 307. The middle section, thus, is the longest. These divisions are more or less arbitrary ones. Some for example, may divide it into four sections, keeping Iago's soliloquy as a section by itself.

The scene rouses various emotions in the reader. It begins with dramatic suspense about the fate of the ships and also ends with dramatic suspense, for the reader becomes apprehensive about Cassio's fate and also inquisitive about how his dismissal will be brought about. As can be seen, Shakespeare has created dramatic suspense in this and the foregoing scene by means of soliloquies, which is not the case with his other plays usually. The soliloquies of Hamlet are of great importance but they are used to reveal Hamlets's character, not to create suspense. Here it is used for both the purposes. The function of the soliloquies has been discussed in more details later on (*vide* Iago's character, in Chapter 7 *infra*).

Act II, scene ii

This scene contains only eleven lines and is the second shortest scene in the play. It can be considered as a link scene or a transitional scene, consisting only of a proclamation issued by Othello and read aloud by a Gentleman. Othello has received the news of the destruction of the Turkish fleet and declares a time for general celebration till eleven o'clock. These festivities are also meant to celebrate his marriage. The proclamation is in prose and prepares the right kind of background for Cassio to get drunk and disorderly so as to get himself dismissed. It is linked thus, to the next scene as well as to the preceding ones. Though in itself it is not important, it provides the link between the first and the third scenes. It is a functional scene, not a useless one.

Act II, scene iii

This is an important scene as it is in this one that Cassio gets himself dismissed. It should be borne in mind that that scene is located in a hall within the castle in which Othello and Desdemona also have their accommodation. The noise made by the revellers could quite possibly disturb them, and the alarm bell certainly would.

It opens with Othello telling Cassio to supervise guard duty and Cassio agrees, telling him that Iago has already done the work but that he too will see to it. Then Othello and Desdemona retire.

Iago enters and there is a dialogue between him and Cassio in which he tries to find out Cassio's sentiments towards Desdemona. Then he invites Cassio to a drinking bout which the latter refuses, saying he has a weak head. Then Cassio allows himself to be lured to meet some young men whom Iago has brought. This gives Iago the chance to deliver his third soliloquy. He knows that if he can make Cassio drink a little more then he will become quarrelsome and start some sort of trouble. So when Cassio enters with some others he shows himself to be a convivial person, starting to sing and calling for drinks. Cassio is made thoroughly drunk; when he leaves the stage Iago maligns him to Montano and the others, telling them that being drunk and disorderly but a regular feature in Cassio.

Then Roderigo enters and Iago prompts him to pick a quarrel with Cassio. Within a few minutes cries for help are heard and Roderigo runs in, driven by Cassio at the point of the sword. Then Montano tells Cassio he is drunk and Cassio, highly offended, starts fighting him. As Bradley has pointed out, there is something ridiculous about the whole business:

> He gets drunk—not disgustingly so, but ludicrously so.[18]

While they are fighting Iago sends Roderigo out to ring the alarm. He himself is pretending to control Cassio all the time. Then the alarm bell rings. M.C. Bradbrook has interpreted this very imaginatively:

> It is the signal that tragedy has begun, for Cassio is doomed by it, and it breaks in on Othello's marriage night like a tocsin.[19]

The ringing of the bell brings Othello to the place, as Iago had known it would, and by this time Montano has got seriously hurt. Othello asks Iago what the matter is and Iago, pretending to be most reluctant, tells the tale so artfully as to make it seem he is trying his best to minimise Cassio's part in the whole affair. Then Othello dismisses Cassio:

> Cassio, I love thee,
> But never more be officer of mine.[20]

Now only Cassio and Iago are left on the stage. Cassio is stone cold sober now, and in a highly dejected mood. He does not remember how Roderigo had picked a quarrel with him and can only blame himself for it. Iago tells him not to despair and to approach Desdemona to speak to Othello for him. This is good advice and Cassio appreciates it and leaves the stage, to enable Iago to deliver his fourth soliloquy.

The major part of this soliloquy is devoted to self-justification. He says nobody will call him a villain for having counselled Cassio to request Desdemona to plead for him. It is but offering friendly advice. We see the gradual formation of his plan in this speech and in his analysis Harold Bloom has observed:

> Harold C. Goddard called Iago a "moral pyromaniac" and we can hear Iago setting fire to himself throughout the play, but particularly in this speech.[21]

After this soliloquy, Roderigo enters. He has spent nearly all his money and wants to return to Venice. Iago persuades him to stay on at Cyprus and then when Roderigo leaves the stage, delivers his fifth soliloquy.

It is a short soliloquy in which he plans out his future course of action. His wife is to ask Desdemona to plead for Cassio to Othello and he will manage things in such a way that Othello might see Cassio requesting Desdemona. He ends the soliloquy and the scene with a Senecan couplet advising not to delay but to strike the iron while it is hot.

As far as versification is concerned, the scene has great variety. First of all it contains both verse and prose. The dialogue between Cassio and Iago in the beginning is in prose, Iago's speech in between the two songs is in prose, then Cassio's speech when he is drunk, is also in prose. Then the dialogue between Iago and Cassio after the exit of Othello and the others is in prose. There is another prose passage by Roderigo.

Apart from all these prose passages, this scene has two songs. These are the first songs in the play. Both are drinking songs, both sung by Iago. As they are sung by but one person throughout, they do not contain refrains. Shakespeare has thus provided great variety in this scene from the metrical point of view.

The scene is firmly linked to the foregoing scene in that in the preceding scene there is a proclamation of general revelries and in this we see the characters sing and drink. It is linked to the next scene in that in it Cassio's dismissal takes place and in the following scene Cassio is to sue Desdemona to speak for him. Indeed, the seeds of tragedy are sown in this scene.

It can be divided into four sections. The first section contains sixty lines, going on till the end of Iago's soliloquy and the entrance of Cassio, Montano and others. Then the second section shows us the revelry and Cassio's dismissal in line 250. The third section consists of the dialogue between Iago and Cassio (l. 326). Then with the exit of Cassio the fourth section begins and lasts till the end. The scene is remarkable in that it contains no less than three soliloquies by Iago.

Usually soliloquies slow down a scene by holding up the action, but this scene is so long and contains so many events that in spite of three soliloquies it remains an eventful scene.

It is a significant scene also in that it concludes Act II. The action has truly started in this Act. All the characters (excepting Lodovico) have been introduced. The action is still in an embryonic stage. Indeed, some critics are of the opinion that it is with the temptation scene (Act II, sc. iii) that the action truly begins, but, as a matter of fact, the foundations for the temptation scene are laid in this one, with Cassio's ignominious dismissal. Iago's plot hinges on this dismissal.

Act III, scene i

This scene is located in front of the castle. Cassio has brought a troupe of singers and musicians and hopes to please Othello and Desdemona by playing music to them. A Clown has also come and this produces a dialogue that provides comic relief. Cassio sends a message to Emilia through him. Then Iago comes and a bit later Emilia comes with a message from Othello. This message is disappointing since it merely says that Othello cannot take Cassio back. The refusal is worded very mildly. Cassio pleads with Emilia to give him a chance to speak to Desdemona and Emilia takes him inside the castle. The scene ends here. It is a very short scene.

The scene, comprising only 56 lines, is half in prose and half in verse, for up till l. 29 (when Iago enters) it is in prose. Though short, it falls into two clear-cut divisions, the prose part constituting the first section and Cassio's dialogues with Iago and Emilia making up the second.

The Act thus begins quietly, with Cassio trying to reinstate himself. The scene takes the action a step forward in his attempts to do so.

Act III, scene ii

This is the shortest scene of the play, containing only six lines. It is to be considered as a link-scene or a transitional one, coming in between and joining the two halves of the play. Othello is seen carrying on his administrative duties, like a conscientious and efficient ruler, as he is holding the post of the governor.

The scene consists of two short speeches by Othello and two half lines spoken by Iago and the Gentlemen attending upon Othello.

The scene, however, occupies a crucial position in the play. *Othello* contains (in this edition) fifteen scenes in all, and this is the eighth. In other words, it is the central scene of the play. Usually this position is given to an important scene, yet here it has been given to an unimportant one. It must be remembered that scene-divisions were very fluid in Elizabethan times. Most of the time it was the director or the stage manager who decided the scene-divisions. Later the different editors also exercised the same liberty. So it will be wrong to declare which is the central scene. In the text being used, it is the central one.

Act III, scene iii

This is the longest scene of the play, and is generally known as the Temptation scene. This phrase is sometimes applied to the entire scene, and sometimes only to that section of the scene where the actual temptation is taking place. It is known as such because it is in this one that Iago first sows the seeds of jealousy in Othello's mind. It is, therefore, a very important scene.

It opens with a dialogue between Desdemona and Cassio in which the former assures the latter of trying her best to reinstate him. Then Othello comes in and Cassio excuses himself. Iago begins his attack with two suggestions. "Ha, I like not that" and that Cassio had "slunk away so guilty-like" on seeing Othello. These hints fail because at once Desdemona starts pleading for

Cassio in a very direct manner. She reminds him of how Cassio used to accompany him during his courting of Desdemona, and would always praise him. Othello agrees to take him back and then Desdemona and Emilia leave the stage.

Now the sequence known as the temptation scene starts, Iago does it very cunningly pretending as if he is most reluctant to say anything against Cassio. He is the one who first mentions jealousy:

O, beware jealousy;
'Tis the green-ey'd monster, which doth mock
That meat it feeds on.[22]

Then Iago mentions social conventions—that it is usual for Venetians to indulge in this kind of light-hearted love-affairs. This is a very clever move on his part as Othello has no knowledge of these matters. Then he brings forth the suggestion that Desdemona can be a hypocrite;

She did deceive her father, marrying you.[23]

This line directly echoes Brabantio's parting words to Othello, and both he and the reader remember them;

Look to her, Moor, have a quick eye to see:
She did deceive her father, may do thee.[24]

Having sown this seed in Othello's mind, Iago next makes a poisonous suggestion—that Desdemona's love for him is unnatural because he is no sophisticated Venetian but a Moor. Her infatuation has worn off and Cassio being a countryman of the same social class, she has turned to him. Then, after having told Othello to observe her behaviour he withdraws, to allow him to deliver his first soliloquy. He has three of them.

The seeds that Iago has sown have fallen on fertile soil, for he is already jealous. His social inferiority has a lot to contribute and so has the difference in age between him and Desdemona.

Haply for I am black,
And have not those soft parts of conversation
That clamberers have, or for I am declin'd
Into the vale of years.[25]

Iago had made three suggestions and two of them are already working. The third suggestion, that love-affairs are commonplace among Venetians, has not yet come to the front. The very fact that Othello has allowed Iago to speak disparagingly of Desdemona speaks volumes because it implies that jealousy is dormant in his character.

After this soliloquy, Desdemona and Emilia enter. They have come to call Othello to his dinner. Othello tells Desdemona that he has a pain in his forehead. What he means is that he is going to grow the horns that cuckolds have, or are supposed to have. Desdemona, of course, does not take in this innuendo and takes out her handkerchief to bind his head. It is too small, and she, without knowing, drops it. Then husband and wife go out together and Emilia picks it up. She tells us that, for some unknown reason, Iago had often asked her to steal it.

Just after this speech, Iago himself comes in and is overjoyed to get the handkerchief. Then Emilia goes away and he delivers his sixth soliloquy. He says that he will plant it in Cassio's rooms, so that he may later tell Othello that Desdemona had given it to Cassio. Then Othello enters and before addressing him, Iago concludes his soliloquy with some of the best lines in this play:

> not poppy, nor mandragora,
> Nor all the drowsy syrups of the world,
> Shall ever medicine thee to that sweet sleep
> Which thou owedst yesterday.[26]

Referring to these lines, Fluchère says:

> Never before had hatred exulted with such accents.[27]

Othello's mind and reason are already going downhill. He has started to talk to himself. He feels that the very reason for his existence has gone. In a splendid speech he bids farewell to his military life:

> Farewell, the tranquil mind, farewell content:
> Farewell the plumed troop, and the big wars,
> That makes ambition virtue: O farewell.[28]

The entire speech is thirteen lines long and is taken to be one of the best passages of Shakespeare. Wilson Knight has called it a "noble apostrophe". Anthony Hecht, however, does not agree. He takes a generally derogatory view of Othello himself as well as of his speeches:

> I think it is tainted nobility: studied, artificial, self-conscious and almost immediately provocative of a parody by Iago.[29]

After this speech Othello demands proof of Desdemona's infidelity and Iago tells him he has seen the handkerchief (which is the first love-token he had given to her) in Cassio's hands. This lie Othello takes for incontrovertible proof and kneels down to take a vow of vengeance. Here occurs another of the famous passages in Shakespeare.

After Othello has taken his vow, Iago also kneels down and vows to help him in his revenge. Othello, as a first step, tells him to kill Cassio within three days and Iago agrees to do so. Here the scene ends.

This is the longest scene in the play, running to 486 lines. It is entirely in verse. Nor does in contain any couplets or songs. From the point of view of prosody, then, there is no variety in the scene. On the other hand, it contains two soliloquies, one by Iago, and Othello's first. It also contains some of the best passages in the play.

The scene can be roughly divided into five sections as follows:

I From Desdemona: "Be thou assured" to Desdemona: "Give thy cause away" (ll. 1-28)

II From Em.: "Madam, here comes" to Des.: "I am obedient" (ll. 29-90)

III From O.: "Excellent wretch" to O.: I'll not believe it (ll. 91-283)

IV From Des.: "How now" to I.: I did say so (ll. 283-334)

V From I.: "Look where he" to the end (ll. 335-485)

The scene, thus, begins quietly, with short sections, and then builds up to a climax in the last climactic scene where both Othello and Iago take their vows. Sometimes in such a long scene, Shakespeare makes the middle section longer than the others, balancing it with two short ones on either side. Here, however, he has not done so. Though the first two sections are much shorter than the middle one, the last two are not noticeably so. But it must be remembered that this kind of dividing into sections is very arbitrary. It is done for the convenience of the reader or the audience.

The scene is almost the central scene of the play and is related to the foregoing and the following ones. The matter of Cassio requesting Desdemona had already been mentioned in Act II, sc. iii. It is related to the following scenes in that we shall see the outcome of jealousy in them. The two aims of Iago, his "double knavery", are achieved in this scene, for he gets the post that had been occupied by Cassio, and he ruins Othello's peace of mind forever. The handkerchief, also, is introduced in it.

Act III, scene iv

It is in this scene that the importance of the handkerchief is brought home to Desdemona as well as to the audience. The scene begins quietly but in an ominous manner because Desdemona is seeking Cassio out to tell him that she has pleaded for him. Before Cassio comes, however, Othello enters. After a few lines of dialogue Othello pretends that he has caught a cold and asks for Desdemona's handkerchief. The one she gives him is not the one he wants. She tells him she does not have that particular handkerchief with her at present and then Othello tells her terrifying things about it.

He tells her that it is a very magical handkerchief which had been given to his mother by an Egyptian enchantress. The peculiar virtue of the handkerchief is that so long as a woman has it in her possession her husband will love her but if she loses it or gives it away then he will loathe her. His mother had given it to him when she died and told him to give it to his wife. She should take great care of it:

> Make it a darling, like your precious eye,
> To lose, or give't away, were such perdition
> As nothing else could match.[30]

This disclosure, not unnaturally, strikes terror into Desdemona's heart. She says she wishes she had not seen it at all. Othello asks if it is lost and demands to see it. She, all unknowingly adds fuel to the fire of his jealousy by pleading for Cassio repeatedly:

Othello: Fetch me that handkerchief, my mind misgives

Desdemona: Come, come,
You'll never meet a more sufficient man.

O.: The handkerchief!

D.: I pray, talk me of Cassio.

O.: The handkerchief!

D.: A man that all his time hath founded his good fortunes on your love, Shar'd dangers with you—

O.: The handkerchief!

D.: I' faith, you are to blame.

O.: Zounds! (exit)[31]

By this time, Othello is so perturbed that he can hardly speak in a connected manner. Desdemona is thunderstruck at his behaviour and, as it happens Iago and Cassio enter at this moment. Cassio once more pleads with her to speak for him and she tells him that she has already done so. Then, after talking about Othello's ill-humour, she and Emilia leave the stage.

Cassio is alone on the stage now, and Bianca comes. Cassio gives her the handkerchief and after some more dialogue between them scene comes to its end.

Shakespeare has used both prose and verse in this scene. The scene opens with a dialogue between Desdemona and the Clown which is in prose. Noble characters usually speak in verse, but when they are talking to humble ones they use prose. The Clown's sentences, as they should be, are all witty and full of puns. After the Clown leaves the stage, the rest of the scene is in verse.

The scene is linked to the foregoing scene in that in it Iago obtains Desdemona's handkerchief and decides to plant it in

Cassio's rooms. It has other links also, the most important of which is Desdemona's pleadings for Cassio's reinstatement. It is linked to the later scenes in that we see how Othello's jealousy manifests itself. In the next scene, Othello will hear Cassio talk about Bianca who comes in this scene. He will also see the handkerchief in Bianca's hands in the next scene.

Bianca is a new character introduced in this scene. By this time half the play is over and it is rather late to introduce a new character, but Shakespeare does not go by rules. Coleridge had, once and for all, decided the question.

> A pedant differed from a master in cramping himself with certain established rules, whereas the master regarded rules as always controllable by and subservient to the end.[32]

Often Shakespeare introduces a new character in the last scene, as is the case with Jaques de Boys in *As You Like It*. One character, Lodovico, is still to be introduced. He will come in the next scene.

The scene falls naturally into three sections. The first consists of the prose dialogue between the Clown and Desdemona, and the dialogue between her and Emilia following his exit. The second section commences with the entrance of Othello in l. 27, and continues until Desdemona and Emilia leave (l. 166). The third comprises the rest of the scene, beginning with the entrance of Bianca and going on till the end. This means that the middle section is flanked by two sections of almost the same length—it is a very neatly constructed scene.

The most important event in this scene is the giving of the handkerchief by Cassio to Bianca. Othello is already racked by jealousy and in the next scene this jealousy will be brought to a higher pitch of intensity by the sight of the handkerchief in Bianca's hands. The handkerchief attains symbolic value in this play, symbolizing love as well as chastity. This symbolic value was not realized by Rymer or by Victor Hugo either when they objected to the importance attached to such a humble object.

This scene brings this Act to an end. It is a fitting scene for this function as the third Act is always a crucial one, and in this scene the crucial action, the giving of the handkerchief to Bianca, takes place. There is not much action in this scene, but the Act takes the action several steps forward. Jealousy has been created, Iago's plan has coalesced, suspense has become intensified. The audience wants to know how Othello will be apprised of the fact that the all important handkerchief is in Bianca's hands, and what will his reaction be to it.

Act IV, scene i

The scene opens with a dialogue between Othello and Iago in which, with great cunning, Iago fans the fire of jealousy in Othello. By this time Othello has reached a state of mind in which the contemplation of Desdemona's infidelity is so painful that it produces physical symptoms, that of unconsciousness. Just before he faints, his words do not form even a sentence:

> Pish! Noses, ears and lips. Is't possible?
> —Confession? —Handkerchief? —O devil!
> (*He falls down*).[33]

This is the lowest point in his career. He is usually very eloquent. His eloquence won him Desdemona's love and it is his eloquence that has made G. Wilson Knight call it "the Othello music". Here we see him muttering disjointed words. The warrior, who had looked danger in the face and had not flinched, loses consciousness.

Iago pretends to be solicitously looking after him and Cassio enters. He tells Cassio to go away as the sight of him may enrage Othello and aggravate his condition. Then Othello recovers consciousness and Iago tells him to have patience. He says he will bring Cassio there and Othello shall hear him talking about Desdemona. Othello withdraws.

Then Cassio comes in again. It has been observed that Cassio's coming and going in this scene are rather artificial. Shakespeare has made him come in and go out and again come in according to the convenience of the plot—he comes in just when he is needed and goes out when he is not needed any longer.

Even if Shakespeare has engineered his coming and going according to the exigencies of the plot, it cannot be denied that these do take the action forward. Iago determines, in a short passage, to talk to Cassio of Bianca in such a way that Othello will think they are talking of Desdemona, and this will not only serve as proof, but will also madden him:

> Othello shall go mad,
> And his unbookish jealousy must conster,
> Poor Cassio's smiles, gestures and light behaviour,
> Quite in the wrong.[34]

This is exactly what happens. Iago talks of Bianca to Cassio in a soft voice so that Othello does not hear it. Cassio reacts in the expected manner. The entire dialogue is interspersed with comments from Othello. This part of the scene is known as "the eaves-dropping scene":

> Cas.: Alas, poor caitiff!
> Oth.: Look how he laughs already!
> Ia.: I never knew a woman love man so.
> C.: Alas, poor rogue, I think i'faith she loves me.
> O.: Now he denies it faintly, and laughs it out.
> I.: Do you hear, Cassio?
> O.: Now he importunes him
> To tell it on; go to, well said, well said.[35]

Thus the strange harrowing piece of dramatic irony goes on. Then there is another stroke of luck for Iago, for Bianca comes in and Othello can see the handkerchief in her hand. When she goes out in a temper, Cassio follows her to soothe her and Othello comes out of hiding. The very first sentence he says is an ominous question. "How shall I murder him, Iago?"[36] Iago takes the responsibility of getting rid of Cassio by midnight so Othello is left to the contemplation of what he will be doing to Desdemona. It is Iago who suggests that he strangle her and Othello agrees for the reason Iago gives appeals to him:

> Strangle her in bed, even the bed she hath contaminated.[37]

Then the outside world intervenes in the person of Lodovico who has brought a letter from Venice. This letter commands Othello to go back to Venice, and appoints Cassio as the governor in his stead. While he is reading the letter, Desdemona talks to Lodovico who, being a relative of Brabantio, is her cousin. Othello intervenes during this dialogue and finally strikes her. Lodovico is shocked at this. He thinks that Othello has gone mad and indeed Othello's behaviour does support this idea. Iago, like the villain that he is, encourages Lodovico in whatever he says.

There is a remarkable amount of prose in this scene. Nearly half of the dialogue is in prose. Othello speaks almost entirely in prose. This is particularly noticeable after Cassio and Bianca have gone out. The speech he delivers when he faints is in prose and so is the entire dialogue with Iago. Out of a scene containing 278 lines, nearly a hundred are in prose.

The scene is linked to the forgoing one in that the subject of both is Desdemona's supposed infidelity and Othello's jealousy. The handkerchief also serves as a link between the two. Bianca makes her second appearance in the play with it and talks about. It is also linked to the next scenes, particularly the last one, in that the act of strangling is mentioned here and the actual action takes place in the last. It is also mentioned that they will sup together that night which is again mentioned in the next scene. Othello's ill-treatment of Desdemona is carried on in the next scene.

The scene can be divided into three sections. The first section lasts till the second entrance of Cassio. Then the eavesdropping scene which follows is a section by itself and also contains the dialogue between Othello and Iago, till the entrance of Lodovico *et al* (l. 209). The rest of the scene from l. 210 onwards makes up the third section. The dramatist has balanced the sections very efficiently. The middle section is the longest, having two shorter sections on either side. This is a feature to be noted repeatedly in Shakespeare: he balances, not only the characters, but also such local details as the different divisions into which a scene falls.

The scene is anticipatory in that it prepares us for the last in which the strangling is to take place. It also shows Othello at his worst (*vide*, Chapter 7 *infra*). As an opening scene for an Act it is an extremely effective one.

Act IV, scene ii

This is the scene that contains the famous sequel known as the brothel-scene in which Othello treats Desdemona as if she were a prostitute in a brothel.

It opens with a dialogue between Othello and Emilia, with Othello presenting a most unattractive side of his character. He is spying upon Desdemona and asks Emilia questions regarding her behaviour to Cassio. Emilia naturally defends her mistress very strongly and then Othello sends her to fetch Desdemona. It is from here that the brothel-scene commences. Othello treats Desdemona as if she were a prostitute and Emilia the keeper. He even asks her openly, "are not you a strumpet?" Desdemona is extremely puzzled and hurt, as is but quite natural. Then Othello goes out and there is a short dialogue between Desdemona and Emilia in which Desdemona says she is so hurt that she cannot even weep and asks Emilia to fetch Iago. When Iago comes in, she talks quite frankly to him, telling him of Othello's accusations, and asking for his advice. Iago tells her that it is because of "the business of the state" that Othello is in a foul temper. By this time the bell for supper rings and Desdemona and Emilia go out.

Then Roderigo comes. His last appearance had been in the drinking-scene (Act II, sc. iii) in which he had been instrumental to Cassio's dismissal. After that an entire Act and one scene of the present Act have gone by without his coming upon the stage. He is in a bad mood now, for he has given a lot of money to Iago as well as jewellery which were meant for Desdemona. Now he says he will meet Desdemona and demand the jewellery back from her. Iago is in a fix, but he is extremely quick-witted and turns the anger of Roderigo to advantage. He had promised Othello that he will get rid of Cassio and now he makes use of Roderigo to do this. He tells Roderigo that Cassio is going to Bianca's place for supper and he must kill him as he comes out after supper. He assured Roderigo that he himself will be there to help him. The scene ends with this plot.

The scene has an almost equal amount of prose and verse. All the dialogue till the entrance of Roderigo is in verse and all thereafter in prose. This is fully in keeping with the tone of the play and its spirit, since the earlier part is extremely serious and Roderigo is more or less a comic figure who usually speaks in prose.

Likewise the scene falls into two clear-cut divisions. The first section consists of the verse dialogue till the entrance of Roderigo and the second of the prose dialogue between Iago and Roderigo. Out of the first section a certain part has been separately called the brothel-scene. This consists of the dialogue from l. 24 to l. 96.

Shakespeare has shown the hero in the most unattractive lights in this scene. He has stooped to question Emilia about his wife's conduct and what is more, not believing her when she vouches for Desdemona's character. Then when Desdemona does come in, he treats her as if she were a prostitute. Desdemona, with her inborn nobility and dignity, does not criticise him in front of Emilia. The scene is linked to both the former and the later scene and forms an integral part of the play.

Act IV, scene iii

This is the famous willow-scene in which Desdemona sings a song about a willow, Rymer, who did not like the play at all, and criticised everything about it, does not approve of this scene. He calls it:

> A filthy sort of Pastoral Scene, where the Wedding sheets, and song of Willow, and her Mother's Maid, poor Barbara, are not the lest moving things in this entertainment.[38]

The scene opens after the supper which had been mentioned in the last two scenes. Othello tells Desdemona to get ready for bed and then goes out, along with Lodovico.

Desdemona starts to get ready for bed. She had told Emilia to cover their bed with the same sheets as had been used on their wedding night. Now she asks Emilia to cover her with the same sheets when she dies. There is a fine touch of irony here, for she does not know that she is going to die on those same sheets, that very night.

While she is getting ready for bed she sings the willow song. Emilia is presumably unpinning and brushing out her hair. It is a very domestic scene. The song she sings is one her mother's maid used to sing. Somehow, as she says, it is keeping on haunting her this evening. It is a sad song and ends, ironically, with reference to marital infidelity:

> I call'd my love false love; but what said he then?
> Sing willow, willow, willow:
>
> If I court moe women, you'll couch with moe men.[39]

There are many touches of dramatic irony in this scene. Her eyes are itching and she wants to know whether that means she will weep. Then she asks Emilia whether she would be unfaithful to her husband for the whole world and Emilia says she would. There is a speech by Emilia justifying adultery and ending with a couplet. The scene ends with a Senecan couplet by Desdemona.

Prosodically the scene has great variety for it contains blank verse, prose, a song and couplet. Prose is used for the speech by Emilia is which she says that she is ready to commit adultery if she is given the whole world. The sentiments are ignoble and it is fitting that prose should be their vehicle. There are two Senecan couplets at the end, spoken by Emilia and Desdemona in that order. Then, of course, there is the willow song, which is the third song in the play.

The scene falls into two unequal sequences. The first section consists of only ten lines, till Othello and the others go out. The rest of the scene is one long section. It is unlike Shakespeare to keep the different sections so unequal in length. Perhaps he wanted to emphasize the dialogue between the two female characters and therefore gives it in one long section. Though long it is not tedious as the song comes just in the middle of it.

This scene brings Act IV to its close and it is a very portentous scene. It is integrally related to the play. Moreover, it is the only important scene in the play in which Iago makes no appearance. He does not appear in Act II, sc. ii either, but that is a link-scene in which no character makes an appearance. This scene with its reference to death and adultery prepares the reader for the next Act.

Act V, scene i

The scene shows the success of Iago's machinations. He has brought Roderigo to the street along which Cassio is to pass. It is entirely dark and Roderigo makes a pass at Cassio which is deflected by the latter's coat. Cassio however, also strikes out and wounds his assailant. Then Iago comes in undetected in the darkness, wounds Cassio from behind and runs away. While Cassio and Roderigo are crying for help and for lights Othello enters and realises that Iago has been as good as his word and he too goes away.

Then Lodovico and Gratiano enter. They can hear the cries of both the men but cannot make out anything in the darkness. Then Iago enters with a light. He of course pretends that he has just heard the noise and come. Taking advantage of the partial darkness he stabs Roderigo, giving him his death-wound. He binds Cassio's wound which he had given himself.

While all this is going Bianca enters. Iago at once picks on her as being responsible for the whole business. This becomes all the more plausible when Bianca confesses that Cassio had been her guest that evening.

Then, attracted by all the commotion Emilia enters. Iago sums up the situation for her. This is the interpretation that Lodovico and Gratiano also will accept.

> Cassio has here been set on in the dark,
> By Roderigo, and fellows that are 'scaped,
> He's almost slain and Roderigo dead.[40]

This scene is entirely in verse, containing one Senecan sentence at the end spoken by Iago. It is also, as there is no need to point out, integrally related to the play. It is a short scene, but even then it can be divided into two sections. The first section lasts till the exit of Othello (l. 36) and the rest of the scene makes up the second section. Othello's ominous parting words ("strumpet, I come") prepares us for the next scene which will be the last.

The play's tragic end is now within sight. Roderigo's is the first death in it. As a matter of fact there are comparatively few deaths in this play than in many Jacobean tragedies. There are only four deaths in it whereas in *The Duchess of Malfi*, for example, there are ten.

The scene highlights the villainy of Iago. He not only wounds Cassio from behind but also stabs Roderigo, killing him. With great presence of mind, he takes command of the situation, binds up Cassio's wound, sends him away to the doctor, sends Emilia to tell Othello of what has happened, etc., etc. It is a most eventful scene.

Act V, scene ii

This is the last and the second longest scene of the play. It opens in a very solemn manner, with Othello entering with a candle and justifying the murder he is going to commit. This opening speech has been much commented upon. It is the second of his three soliloquies. Stanley Cavell is of the opinion that he is in a dazed condition:

> Othello must mean that he is acting impersonally, but the words are those of a man in a trance, in a dream-state.[41]

He kisses Desdemona and when she wakes up asks her to confess. This pious act is usually done by a priest but as Othello is going to kill her, he asks her to confess on her own. Then he asks her if she had had a love-affair with Cassio and tells her that Cassio is dead now. When she persists in saying that she is innocent he strangles her.

Almost immediately Emilia calls from beyond the closed door. Now Othello delivers his third soliloquy in which practical considerations are mingled with grief. He knows Emilia has come to tell him of Cassio's death and she is sure to speak to his wife. The thought makes him cry out that he has no wife now:

> My wife, my wife, my wife; I ha' no wife; O, insupportable!
> O heavy hour![42]

He then opens the door to Emilia. She tells him that Roderigo has been killed but Cassio still lives. At this point Desdemona speaks.

As a matter of fact she speaks thrice. In this she is like Webster's Duchess in *The Duchess of Malfi*. She too had been strangled, but she speaks twice, both the times a single word. Desdemona speaks thrice and each time she speaks sentences:

> O falsely, falsely murder'd!
> ... ...
> A guiltless death I die.
> Em.: O, who hath done this deed?
> Des.: Nobody, I myself, farewell:
> Commend me to my kind lord, O, farewell! [43]

These lines have been praised as well as adversely criticised. They have been praised because of their dramatic effectiveness, for the economical way in which Shakespeare makes Emilia aware of her murder and for the light they shed on Desdemona's character. They have, contrariwise, been criticised for being unrealistic and melodramatic. Way back in the seventeenth century, Rymer had satirically remarked:

> We may learn here that a Woman never loses her Tongue even though after she is stifled.[44]

Now that Emilia has become aware of the fact that Othello, out of jealousy has murdered Desdemona, she goes to the root of the matter at once. She exposes Iago for the villain that he is, and also tells Othello about the handkerchief—how Iago had told her to get it, how she had picked it up when Desdemona had dropped it and had given it to him (Act III, sc. iii). By this time Montano, Gratiano, Iago and others have come in and Emilia exposes Iago's villainy to all of them. Iago stabs Emilia and tries to escape but is caught.

Lodovico assumes command of the situation. He divests Othello of his powers and appoints Cassio in his place. Othello then delivers his famous last speech (which has been criticised adversely by Eliot) and kills himself. He totters to the bed and kisses Desdemona before he dies. Thus he begins the scene with a kiss and ends his life with one.

The scene ends with a speech by Lodovico in which he assigns everyone his duties. Iago is to be punished, Gratiano is to take care of the house and Cassio, as the governor, is to enforce the punishment of Iago. He himself will go to Venice to explain all that has happened.

The scene is entirely in verse, indeed, prose would have been out of place in it as it is the last scene of a tragedy and the pitch of the entire scene is very high. Prose passages would have lowered the pitch. This could have been admitted in any other scene, but not in the last one.

It is a long scene, the second longest in the play, comprising 372 lines, and can be divided into four sections. The first of them lasts till the entrance of Emilia (l. 107). The second goes on till the entrance of Montano and others (l. 169). The third continues till the death of Othello (l. 357). The rest of the play makes up one section. The third is the longest section. It is in this section that the exposition of Iago's villainy, the death of Emilia and, most important, Othello's own death, take place. The last section, which concerns matters of administration and consists mainly of the speech of Lodovico, is the shortest. It is the shortest, but quite important, as it restores moral order in Cyprus.

The structure of this last scene has been anaylsed by many critics. Nevill Coghill finds it to be a neat, well-plotted scene:

> Othello may still seem "an honorable murderer". The structure of the last scene is designed to help in this; it is symmetrically planned. It begins and ends in an attempt at an act of Justice, on a kiss.[45]

Three of the four deaths in Othello occur in this scene. Out of them the death of the hero generates pity and terror in the heart of the audience, as indeed, does the death of the heroine also. But Emilia's death should not be neglected. She gives her life for Desdemona and her death is by far the noblest.

References

1. Act I, scene i, ll. 96-98, p. 8.
2. Ridley, M.R., *op.cit.*, pp. xlix-xlx.
3. *Ibid.*
4. Hecht, Anthony, *Othello*, in Bloom, Harold, ed. *Modern Critical Interpretations of Othello*, Delhi, Worldview Pubs., 1987, p. 124.
5. Act I, scene ii, l. 59, p. 19.
6. Act I, scene ii, ll. 98-99, p. 20.
7. Act I, scene iii, ll. 167-69, p. 31.

8. Act I, scene iii, ll. 292-93, p. 39.
9. Ridley, M.R., *op.cit.*, p. 45 fn.
10. Act I, scene iii, ll. 401-02, p. 46.
11. Wain, John, *op.cit.*, p. 53.
12. Knight, G. Wilson, *op.cit.*, p. 111.
13. Ridley, *op.cit.*, p. 54 fn.
14. *Ibid.*
15. Act II, scene i, ll. 122-24, p. 55.
16. Act II, scene i, ll. 306-08, p. 67.
17. Act II, scene i, ll. 184-93, pp. 59-60.
18. Bradley, *op.cit.*, p. 195.
19. Bradbrook, M.C., *Themes and Conventions of Elizabethan Tragedy*, Cambridge, the University Press, 1969 rpt., p. 20.
20. Act II, scene iii, ll. 239-40, p. 81.
21. Bloom, Harold, *op.cit.*, p. 4.
22. Act III, scene iii, ll. 169-71, p. 103.
23. Act III, scene iii, l. 210, p. 105.
24. Act I, scene iii, ll. 292-93, p. 39.
25. Act III, scene iii, ll. 267-70, p. 109.
26. Act III, scene iii, ll. 335-38, p. 113.
27. Fluchère, Henri, *Shakespeare*, London, Longmans, Green & Co. Ltd., 1953, p. 225.
28. Act III, scene iii, ll. 353-55, p. 114.
29. Hecht, Anthony, *Othello*, in Bloom, *op.cit.*, p. 132.
30. Act III, scene iv, ll. 64-66, p. 127.
31. Act III, scene iv, ll. 87-95, pp. 128-29.
32. Coleridge, *Report of a Lecture at Bristol* (Nov. 1813) in Wain, *op.cit.*, p. 54.
33. Act IV, scene i, ll. 42-43, p. 137.
34. Act IV, scene i, ll. 100-03, p. 141.
35. Act IV, scene i, ll. 108-14, p. 142.
36. Act IV, scene i, l. 166, p. 145.
37. Act IV, scene i, ll. 203-04, p. 146.
38. Wain, *op.cit.*, p. 43.
39. Act IV, scene iii, ll. 54-56, p. 166.
40. Act V, scene i, ll. 111-13, p. 176.
41. Bloom, *op.cit.*, p. 14.

42. Act V, scene ii, ll. 98-99, p. 183.
43. Act V, scene ii, ll. 118, 123-26, pp. 184-85.
44. Wain, *op.cit.*, p. 45.
45. *Ibid.*, p. 153.

6

The Major Themes

A play, in order to gain the status of a work of art, must, in addition to other features, have a unifying theme. The plot might observe all the classical rules and yet the play itself will give an impression of fragmentariness if this feature is lacking. The dramatist ought to have a cogent and coherent idea to convey to the reader or the audience. This idea might embody an abstruse philosophical concept, a clear moral message, or, even, an aesthetic idea. The processes of creation vary with each individual and sometimes the writer may have a theme in his mind from the beginning. Sometimes, on the other hand, he may start with the vague idea of just telling a story and then gradually a central theme will emerge as he writes. This is what most frequently happens in novels and plays. As is most often the case with Shakespeare, the writer's intentions may not be known to the reader and he finds the unifying theme only after close study. In that case different readers will put their own interpretations upon the play, as has happened with our dramatist. His mature plays have given rise to many interpretations and even *Othello*, which would seem to be quite a simple play from this point of view, has given rise to quite a few of them. This variety in critical opinions does not mean that the work is vague, and aimless. Quite the opposite in fact, for multiplicity of meanings implies that the work itself is rich and complex. In addition there is another factor that adds to the complexity. There might be one central theme and several subsidiary ones, but there might also be certain ideas that are important and so recur again and again. The French critic Henri Fluchère has pointed out:

> There are minor themes, ceremonial themes, major themes, symbolic themes; sometimes set out *en Clair*, sometimes developed at length and sometimes on the contrary, just suggested.[1]

All these factors have to be kept in mind when discussing the themes in any Shakespearean play. We shall now cast a glance at the rich variety of themes to be found in *Othello*.

(a) The Theme of Christian Belief

This is the view of H.W. Wilson. As it is, he has divided Shakespeare's tragedies into two categories: (i) the Order of Faith and (ii) the Order of Nature. *Othello* comes within the first group. Here, along with *Othello*, he has put *Romeo and Juliet*, *Macbeth* and *Hamlet* also. Again within this category there are two more; (a) Thesis and (ii) Antithesis. *Othello* falls within the second. Explaining the first of these groups, i.e., those plays that sow the Order of Faith he says that they

> invoke Christian assumptions; indeed, they can hardly be discussed without some reference to a specifically Christian way of thought.[2]

Referring to *Othello* in particular, Wilson says that in it the evil that exits is man-made. It has to be understood against the perspective of Christian faith;

> *Othello* is concerned with the Christian belief in sin and punishment.[3]

This, according to him, is the central theme of the play. When Othello kills Desdemona, it is because she has sinned and has to be punished killing her is an act of justice and this is exactly how Othello looks upon it. His love for her endures, but all the same she has to die.

Conversely, when he realises that he has killed an innocent person, along with the most intense grief there also comes the realisation that he has sinned and has to be punished. Desdemona's death has to have its counterpart in his own death, and he stabs himself. He does not pause to consider that it is forbidden in Christian religion to take one's own life. He is no Hamlet. He is a man of violent passions and quick decisions. So, after delivering his speech he commits suicide.

This happens right at the end. Before that, in the entire play, Shakespeare judges man by the degree of selfishness he exhibits. There is a core of selfishness in all of us, we have a tendency to put our own ego before anything else, and that is the Original Sin:

> ...the core of selfishness, of self-regard that is in all of us, that is one aspect of "original sin"—the putting of oneself before God and one's own fellowman.[4]

This is a very serious attitude that the critic has taken, because if the fact of sin and punishment is there in life, there is also the pact of repentance. Christianity says that the wages of sin is death, but it also says that those who repent will be forgiven. There is no doubt that Othello repents. The serious student should keep his mind open. It is true that Iago does not repent and therefore Iago should be punished. But Othello puts himself beyond God's forgiveness by taking his own life.

(b) Intellect vs. Humanity

It is G. Wilson Knight's view that Shakespeare is studying the relationship between a disillusioned intellect and good-natured humanity in this play:

> The play turns on this theme: the cynical intellect pitted against a lovable humanity transfigured by qualities of heroism and grace.[5]

It is Iago of course who represents cynical intelligence and Othello loving humanity. Iago's attitude is made clear quite early in the play. When Desdemona asks him his opinion of her he says:

> O gentle lady, do not put me to't
> For I am nothing, if not cirtical.[6]

He is thus, a self-confessed cynic, but he gives evidence of his cynicism earlier in the play when he tells Roderigo that Desdemona will soon tire of Othello and look around her for a lover:

> Virtue? a fig! 'tis in ourselves that we are thus, or thus.... It cannot be that Desdemona should long continue her love unto the moor.
> ....She must have change, she must.[7]

Shakespeare has pitted this man, who is all cynicism, against Othello who is a passionate lover and a brave, idealistic soldier. They have nothing in common. So when Iago brings his suspicions about her, Othello succumbs to it. It should be remembered that Iago does this very cleverly. He starts with hints and insinuations and then gradually goes on to build up a case against her. When Othello demands proof he is ready with the handkerchief and engineers his conversation with Cassio in such a way that it supports him. He has been very lucky in the play, every coincidence serving to support him. He really believes that Desdemona will soon tire of Othello. Fidelity, loyalty, virtue, these are concepts foreign to his nature. It is easy for him to weave his web of treachery for this something he truly believes in. He is, as he thinks, merely speeding up the inevitable betrayal of Othello by Desdemona. He makes it clear in his very first soliloquy. Knight says:

> Iago first states his disbelief in Othello's and Desdemona's continued love and next thinks of a way of precipitating its end. That is, he puts his cynicism into action.[8]

Thus from the very beginning the theme is stated and the entire play then proceeds to enact it. Against this cynical intellect, Othello has no defence. He succumbs with hardly a struggle. It is true that in the end both the hero and the villain perish, but that is how it should be in a tragedy.

(c) Noble man enduring a shock

According to A.C. Bradley, this is a theme that recurs in Shakespeare. *Hamlet* shows his first treatment of it and *Othello* the second. Comparing Hamlet with Othello he says:

> ...each is a man exceptionally noble and trustful, and each endures the shock of a terrible disillusionment.[9]

The fact that Othello is noble and trustful is self-evident. His nobility expresses itself from the moment he enters the stage, and this in spite of the picture previously built up by Iago.

In the previous scene (Act I, sc. i), Iago had built up the picture of an opinionated, blusterous, vain man, but the audience is taken by surprise when he does come upon the stage. He is dignified and does not talk much. It is Iago who does the talking in the beginning. When Othello does speak he shows himself to be a dignified man of judgment and not boastful. He knows his own worth and there is no need to boast about it.

This dignity is endangered only when he is attacked by Iago. He has repeatedly told us that his love for Desdemona is an all-consuming passion that he will not be able to exist without it. Iago's insinuations rock the very foundations of his existence and finally cut them away. It is only then that he talks disjoined prose, in the first scene of the fourth Act.

But, once he has taken the decision to kill Desdemona he recovers his poise and his nobility. He opens the murder scene with one of the best passages in Shakespeare and brings his own life to a close wit another. Both of these passages have been much commented upon and T.S. Eliot is the only critic who calls their nobility into question. Even then, he calls Othello's state of mind into question, not the passage itself.

Othello is also very trustful and trusts "honest Iago" up to the hilt. Iago has already got a reputation for honesty:

> A man he is of honesty and trust
> To his conveyance I assign my wife.[10]

So when Iago starts his hints and insinuations, Othello believes in them. Noble natures are generally trustful. They themselves are incapable of duplicity and evil designs, so they cannot conceive of it in others. It must, moreover, be remembered that Iago sets about his business in a very cunning manner. All the time he pretends reluctance and also pretends to defend Desdemona whereas he is doing the opposite. The most blatant of such passages of false defence is this:

> Or to be naked with her friend in bed,
> An hour or more, not meaning any harm.[11]

Othello is too noble to perceive what Iago is doing. When he has convinced Othello of Desdemona's infidelity and Othello has taken his vows to avenge himself, he too takes an equally solemn vow to help him. This does but strengthen Othello's trust in him. This trust endures till the very end. It is only when Emilia discloses the actual facts about the fateful handkerchief that he is finally convinced.

This, as Bradley says "exceptionally noble and trustful" man's confrontation with the fact that his wife has betrayed him, destroys him. His love for her made up the very substance of his life. So, "chaos is come again" for him. As Bradley has pointed out, very much the same thing happens to Hamlet, Lear and Timon of Athens. He groups these plays together as treating the same theme.

(d) Tearing down of Privacy

John Bayley has classified the play as one of the "tragedies of privacy" (*vide* Chapter 4 *supra*) and, thus, declares that "the tearing down of privacy" is the theme of *Othello*:

> ...the theme perennial; the tearing down of privacy is a subject which fits our age, as it might fit any age.[12]

This critic concentrates on Desdemona's love for Othello. She had fallen in love with him when she heard him eloquently talking about his adventure. In the beginning she heard him in patches, in between the intervals of her household work:

> But still the house affairs would draw her thence;
> Whichever as she could with haste dispatch,
> She'd come again, and with greedy ear
> Devour up my discourse.[13]

Later she made time for herself to listen to Othello without any break. This telling and listening created a private world of their own. In this private world, Othello is not the respected general he is to others. Here he is just the husband of Desdemona. Like a good wife she has to take care of him, see to it that he eats properly and wears gloves to keep himself warm. It is a world of husband and wife—a private world.

What Iago does, what the form of tragedy does, is to destroy this privacy. This tearing down of privacy is the theme of *Othello*. The private world of love is built up in the beginning and then gradually destroyed. This critic also differentiates between different concepts of love as applied to the three main characters. It is an ennobling idealistic passion for Othello. For Desdemona love and lust are inextricably mingled. Iago looks upon it as just lust. These different attitudes help in creating and destroying the private world of husband and wife. This is a bit different from domestic tragedy.

(e) Vulnerability of Love

Othello usually makes a pair with *Romeo and Juliet*, known as the Italian tragedies. In both, the prime cause of tragedy is love. In the former, we have a pair of young lovers who are persecuted by fate. In the latter, we have a pair of lovers who are more mature. Desdemona is young, but Othello is middle-aged, as he himself is aware of:

> I am declin'd
> Into the vale of years.[14]

The real difference between the two tragedies lies in the fact that in the former the vulnerability of love is shown by attacks from outside. This attack is so strong that the lovers cannot survive it. In *Othello* the situation is reversed. Here the attack is from inside. Here also, however, the lovers cannot survive the attack:

> Shakespeare's two Italian tragedies offer companion pictures of the vulnerability of love, threatened outside in *Romeo and Juliet*, from within in *Othello*.[15]

This is perfectly true, for, had the seeds of tragedy, which is the result of jealousy, not been dormant in Othello's mind, Iago's insinuations would have failed. Othello is a man of action, a warrior with a high sense of honour. Such a man would not have tolerated Iago's hints. More likely he would have fetched a cuff at Iago's head at the very first hint. Instead he wants to know what Iago meant by it. The temptation scene in nearly two hundred lines long and when by the end of it Iago leaves, Othello is in the throes of inferiority complex as well as jealousy:

> Haply, for I am black,
> And have not those soft parts of conversation
> That chamberers have, or for I am diclin'd
> Into the vale of years.[16]

There are three points over which he has inferiority complex. Firstly he is black, secondly he does not have social graces and thirdly he is middle-aged and therefore too old for Desdemona. The combination of these three failings has served to make him very unsure of himself. In contrast, Cassio is a highly personable young man and belongs to the same social circle as Desdemona does. So Iago's hints fall on fertile soil. Here there are no external obstacles in the way of union, for union has been achieved in the very beginning of the play. The process of disintegration is what is shown here and this disintegration comes through the extremely credulous nature of the hero. His love is vulnerable from within. What Iago says earlier is very true of Othello:

> 'tis in ourselves that we are thus, or thus.[17]

The seeds of jealousy and therefore of tragedy already are there in Othello. When, seeing the success of his first tentative attempts, Iago becomes more explicit and talks of jealousy, he meets with no opposition. Thus, if we compare *Othello* with *Romeo and Juliet* we see that whereas in the earlier play all the obstacles in the ways of union came from outside the exact opposite happens in this play. Here union is achieved in the beginning, but then obstacles are generated within the mind of Othello. In any case, love is shown to be extremely vulnerable in both:

> It is this concentration on vulnerable love that distinguishes these plays from two others where love comes to grief, *Troilus and Cressida* and *Antony and Cleopatra*.[18]

(f) Marital Love

The Shakespearean critic Carol Thomas Neely divides the critics of *Othello* into three groups: (a) those who attack Othello, or "Othello critics", (b) those who attack Iago, or "Iago critics" and (c) those who find a different cause for the tragic outcome of the play. She puts herself within this third group and finds a conflict in marital love the root cause and the theme of the play:

> I argue that the play's central theme is love—specifically marital love—that its central conflict is between the men and the women.[19]

After this she gives us analyses of all the characters, showing how there is conflict in each of them. Thus in Othello, there is conflict between idealistic love and lust. In Iago, there is conflict between cynicism and reluctant admiration for the principal characters. He, in his own way, pays tribute to Othello's "constant, noble, loving nature"[20] and to Cassio's "daily beauty in his life"[21], and to Desdemona's "blest condition".[22] Roderigo shows a combination of romanticism, and misogyny, Cassio idealises "the divine Desdemona" and denigrates Bianca. There is conflict in each of the characters.

Against this, the female characters are far more balanced. All three of them take a far more balanced view of men than the men do themselves:

> From the start they, like the comedy heroines, combine realism with romance, mocking with affection.[23]

The conflict between men and women in the play lies in this: the men are, finally, unable to turn the woman's virtue into vice and the women too are unable to cure men of their fantasies. Rosalind cures Orlando of his impractical idealism in *As You Like It* and the play ends with marriage. Here the conflict remains and the play ends in tragedy.

This particular view may not be shared by all and may be called far-fetched. Shakespeare's plays are so complex that they have given rise to, and will continue to do so, to hundreds of critical ideas.

(g) Reason vs. Instinct

This is a far more plausible view than the one given above. M.R. Ridley argues that the instinct of Othello is far more reliable than his reason:

> If I were challenged to provide a "theme" for *Othello* I should suggest "Reason vs. Instinct".[24]

Othello is a man more of instinct than of reason and therefore, whenever he depends upon his instinct he is right. Whenever he ratiocinates about it however, he is in the wrong. Again and again in the play this is clearly borne out. His instinct prompts him to distrust Iago but the rational part of him believes:

If she be false, O, then heaven mocks itself,
I'll not believe it.[25]

This is Othello's instinct speaking. But, then, he reasons and it produces doubts:

I think my wife be honest, and think she is not,
I think that thou art just and think thou art not.[26]

Here he quite clearly uses the word "think". At other places he does not openly use this particular word but it is quite clear that it is his rational mind that is speaking:

They that mean virtuously, and yet do so,
The devil their virtue tempts, and they tempt heaven.[27]

This is well reasoned and completely wrong. His instinct prompts him again and again not to believe in Iago but it is reason that finally triumphs.

Thus we see that there is great difference of opinion about the theme of the play. Only a few of them have been given here. Thus Kenneth Burke thinks the theme is "disequilibrium of monogamistic love", Arthur Kirsch thinks it is "the polarization of erotic love", Edward Snow finds it to be "the male order of things", Richard Wheeler thinks it is "the conflict among male autonomy, female sexuality and nurturing femininity". All these views are partially true, for nothing can be said to be the last word on Shakespeare.

References

1. Fluchère, *op.cit.*, p. 195.
2. Wilson, *On the Design of Shakespearean Tragedy*, Canada, Univ. of Toronto Press, 1957, p. 3.
3. *Ibid.*, p. 53.
4. *Ibid.*, p. 57.
5. Knight, G. Wilson, *op.cit.*, p. 112.
6. Act II, scene i, ll. 118-19, p. 55.
7. Act I, scene iii, ll. 319-55, pp. 40-43.
8. Knight, *op.cit.*, p. 113.
9. Bradley, A.C., *op.cit.*, p. 142.
10. Act I, scene iii, ll. 283-85, p. 38.
11. Act IV, scene i, ll. 3-4, p. 135.

12. Wain, *op.cit.*, p. 177.
13. Act I, scene iii, ll. 145-50, p. 29.
14. Act III, scene iii, ll. 269-70, p. 109.
15. Snyder, Susan, *Beyond Comedy: Othello,* in Bloom, *op.cit.*, p. 36.
16. Act III, scene iii, ll. 267-70, p. 109
17. Act I, scene iii, ll. 319-20, p. 40.
18. Snyder, S., *op.cit.*, p. 36.
19. Neely, Carol Thomas, *Women and Men in Othello,* in Bloom, *op.cit.*, p. 81.
20. Act II, scene i, l. 284, p. 66.
21. Act V, scene i, l. 19, p. 171.
22. Act II, scene i, l. 247, p. 64.
23. Neely, *op.cit.*, p. 86.
24. Ridley, *op.cit.*, p. lv.
25. Act III, scene iii, ll. 282-83, p. 110.
26. Act III, scene iii, ll. 390-91, p. 117.
27. Act IV, scene i, ll. 7-8, p. 185.

7

The Major Characters

(a) Shakespeare's Characters

Cicero had defined drama as "imitation of life, image of truth, mirror of custom" and the characters in a play can best exemplify all of these qualities. Shakespeare is the acknowledged master in this field. Besides being realistic, convincing human beings they often gain symbolic dimensions, thus gaining universality. Certain dramatists depict their central characters with loyalty to life as well as expertise, but tend to neglect their minor characters. Marlowe is a notable example of this type of dramatist. Our poet, except in his early works, depicts all his characters carefully, giving them individuality, however minor they might be.

In addition to the two features mentioned above, another notable feature about Shakespeare's characterisation is that he has given us more memorable dramatic characters than any one else. The great tragic heroes like Othello and others, the heroines of his comedies, and many others are immortal figures. Others dramatists have given one or two, Shakespeare has given a whole gallery.

What has also to be remembered is that he never reached a point of stagnation. As a whole, there is continuous development in his creative career. His understanding of his fellow creatures grew as he himself matured, and so did his capacity of depicting them. Henri Fluchère has made a very valuable observation in connection with Shakespeare's art of characterisation.

> Shakespeare was indeed all his characters in the sense that he created them out of nothing, brought life into

> them upon the stage, made them speak as they would speak if faced with the situations in which he placed them or with the characteristics that he gave them.[1]

It is but natural that such a miraculous expertise should come with time, it was not there in the beginning. Painstaking observation as well as inborn intuition produced his characters. In the first phase of his career, he was learning his art and the characters show signs of immaturity. The witty lords of *Love's Labour's Lost* can be barely distinguished from each other though even at this stage Lord Berowne has been clearly individualised.

More conscious artistry is seen in every field in the second phase. Here we have the important male figures of the Chronicle Plays and the charming heroines of the golden comedies.

The male figures in the comedies (except for Shylock) are somewhat disappointing as they are overshadowed by heroines of the plays.

It is the third phase of his career that gives us the great male tragic figures. The four great tragedies and the problem comedies were written at this time, presenting a world in which it is evil that predominates, though ultimately it is defeated. The great heroes, Hamlet, Othello, King Lear and Macbeth were created at this time, Lady Macbeth an outstanding figure by any standard, is the most memorable female character of this time.

The last Romances present characters against a completely different perspective, in that these characters take on an almost religious dimension. The chief character undergoes a spiritual journey. He commits sins and then expiates them in long years of suffering and repentance, and finally gains forgiveness. While this process of purification is going on, a purer and more innocent younger generation has grown to maturity to carry on the business of life and procreation.

Though Fluchère says of the characters of Shakespeare that "he created them out of nothing" this is, strictly speaking, not true. Contemporary stage-conventions and philosophical concepts provided a base, as well as classical rules and examples. Rules for characterisation had been laid down by Aristotle, and expounded and exemplified by later critics. As has already been pointed out, he has studied the works of classical dramatists at school. There were also many other works that defined and gave examples of different kinds of characters, like Newton's *The Touchstone of Complexions,* Hall's *Characters of Virtues and Vices*, Sir Thomas Overbury's *Characters,* etc. When in need of a certain character, the dramatist had only to turn to these.

Theophrastus had given more than a hundred of such character-sketches. The tradition had been started by Aristotle who gave sketches of many characters in his *Nichomachaean Ethics*. In *Poetics* he laid down some rules, applicable to all dramatic characters. We shall now have a look at these traits that, according to Aristotle, all characters should have.

There are four of them, (a) Proportion or Goodness (b) Appropriateness (c) Realism and (d) Consistency. The first of these, the quality of Proportion (often translated as goodness), has two implications. The moral intention of any action or speech must be good. He says:

> Any speech or action that manifests itself in moral purpose of any kind will be expressive of character: the character will be good if the purpose is good.[2]

The goodness, as Aristotle points out, is a relative factor, differing with characters of different classes. This concept was later extended to include the existence of evil in a character. Goodness and evil must both exist in a character just as they do in human beings. They must, however, be in proportion. A character may be predominantly good, but some proportion of imperfection must be there in him. This is the reason this quality is sometimes translated as proportion.

The second quality is Appropriateness or Propriety. A character should act or speak in accordance with the kind of person he is:

> There is a type of manly valour; but valour in a woman, or unscrupulous cleverness, is inappropriate.[3]

This rule, usually, is faithfully followed by the Elizabethans. One hardly ever finds a character behaving in an inappropriate manner.

Realism is the third quality. Characters should be true to life. Aristotle carefully points out that this quality is different from both goodness and propriety, but he does not say anything else about it. Shakespeare's characters are always true to life. Their actions and speeches tally with our ideas of what is perfectly natural and realistic. Even when the characters are at a rather high level, as in *Othello,* they are quite realistic.

Aristotle gives great importance to the fourth quality, that of Consistency. A character should remain true to his own nature and must not change drastically. Here, as far as our own play is concerned, one of the critics has brought the charge of what amounts almost to inconsistency in Othello. The matter shall be discussed when his character will be analysed.

In Elizabethan plays, as the foregoing discussion has made clear, the delineation of characters depended on two factors. On the theoretical side, there were the classical rules and on the practical side there were the character-sketches given by the classical and contemporary writers. These were available to everyone. How is it, then, that Shakespeare is the only one who has given us characters who have become part of our lives? He did not defy the age-old rules and contemporary customs. Instead, very often, he turned them to his own advantage.

In addition to all these features there is the towering figure of the tragic hero. Aristotle and his commentators have laid down many specific rules about him. Besides the classical theories, Shakespeare had the practical examples of other tragic heroes in Latin and English plays, specially those of Seneca in Latin and Kyd and Marlowe in English. In addition to the four features outlined above, Aristotle has specified certain other qualities of the tragic hero. He must be better than the average, of noble birth and nature, and he must have some kind of flaw in his nature. Of these, it is the third aspect that is the most important. This has come to be known as "the tragic flaw" which brings inevitable tragic doom. This is how Aristotle describes the tragic hero:

> A man who is not eminently good and just, yet whose misfortune is brought about not by vice or depravity but by some error or frailty.[4]

The Greek word is "hamartia", which essentially means an error of judgment that leads the hero to make a mistake that brings about his downfall. In Elizabethan times it came to encompass a serious shortcoming in the character and not a mere mistake, like ambition in Macbeth or jealousy in the case of our hero, Othello. It need not, in Aristotelian terms, mean a destructive trait. An imperfection that leads a man to commit a crime imperils the nobility of his character. Aristotle takes special care to point out that the flaw in the character is not a serious one, but merely a frailty in a man who is otherwise worthy of respect. He clearly says that the tragic hero must be better than the average so as to inspire respect.

> Tragedy is an imitation of persons who are above the common level.... The poet, in representing men who are irascible or indolent, or have such other defects of character, should present the type and yet ennoble it.[5]

The Elizabethans heightened and intensified this trait so that it would lead that hero to commit a crime, or many crimes (as in the case of Macbeth) to bring tragic doom upon him.

When we turn to the characters of this play, we see that each of them is well-defined and individualistic. Shakespeare's art has reached its full maturity and each major character is a memorable one. The character fall automatically into two groups, the major and the minor ones. Of them Othello, Iago, Desdemona and Cassio will be taken as falling within the first group and the rest into the second. Some critics would count Cassio as a minor character but in the present work he will be treated as belonging to the first group. It is remarkable how few characters Shakespeare has used here. In the list of *Dramatis Personae* only twelve characters are there, whereas in *Hamlet* there are seventeen and in *King Lear* twenty. Again, tragedy in this play affects only a small circle of characters, Othello, Desdemona and Emilia. It affects Iago also for he is ruined, though he does not die. This not only makes the play a domestic tragedy, but intensifies the tragic effect of generating pity and terror.

(b) Othello

From the very beginning indeed, there have been two different attitudes to Othello. There have been those who look upon him with disfavour, and those who idealise him. Rymer, in the seventeenth century belonged to the first of these groups. He called Othello "the Jealous Booby" and "a villainous Blackamoor".[6] This line is later followed by T.S. Eliot and F.R. Leavis and a few others, but there are not many of them.

On the other hand, there are a number of critics who idealise Othello. Dr. Johnson is one:

> The fiery openness of Othello, magnanimous, artless and credulous boundless in his confidence, ardent in his affections, inflexible in his resolution and obdurate in his revenge.[7]

A.C. Bradley and many other Shakespearean critics agree with Dr. Johnson:

> Othello is...by far the most romantic figure among Shakespeare's heroes.
>
> ... ...
>
> He has greater dignity than any other of Shakespeare's men.[8]

Between these two extremes of Rymer and Bradley there are any numbers of analyses of his character. We shall now have a look at the gradual development of his character as seen in the play. He is an ideal Elizabethan hero, though he may not be, by strict standards, an ideal Aristotelian, or classical, hero.

We do not see him in the first scene. This is the case with some other tragic heroes also. As a matter of fact, King Lear is the only hero who appears in the first scene. Hamlet, Macbeth and Othello, all appear later, in the second scene. Othello is absent only in three scenes, Act II, scene i; Act II, scene ii; and Act III, scene i. This is slightly against the Aristotelian rule that the hero must be present in every scene. But then it is well-known that our dramatist is no stickler for rules.

Preparations have been made for his entrance but these preparations are all negative ones. The description given by Iago is an extremely negative one. They have been listed thus:

> He loves his own pride and purpose, he uses bombastic circumstances, he stuffs his speeches with epithets of war, he makes a thoroughly bad appointment out of favouritism, he is an old black ram and a Barbary horse, he is lascivious and an extravagant and wheeling stranger of here and everywhere.[9]

The reader has to judge for himself when he appears.

An impartial judgment shows him to be a highly dignified man who does not talk much, whereas Iago had described a blustery and obstinate person. As the scene goes on the impression of his being a man of action rather than of words deepens. He is fully conscious of his own worth:

> My services, which I have done the seigniory
> Shall out-tongue his complaints.[10]

This is no vain boasting; it is but a statement of fact, borne but by the attitude of the senators. The entire speech is quiet and dignified, but Anthony Hecht who is very much against Othello calls this speech "ludicrous and nervous vanity".[11]

Even while he is talking to Iago, Cassio comes to summon him to the Council. Then comes Brabantio with his attendants to capture him. Then Othello, with but one line, proves his strength and dignity;

> Keep up your bright swords, for the dew will rust them.[12]

Thus, having stopped two parties from fighting, he addresses Brabantio, rebuking him with dignity:

> Good seignor, you shall more command with years
> Than with your weapons.[13]

He really shows himself as a man of few words, and also one who has complete control over himself. This last feature is revealed when, without losing his temper he talks to Brabantio in a cool manner though the former vilifies him. Instead of returning in kind, he asks Brabantio what he wants, and on being told that Brabantio wants him to be put into prison, he puts a very simple question:

> How may the Duke be therewith satisfied,
> Whose messengers are here about my side.[14]

The fact that he is of great importance to the Duke had become clear when Cassio had come with the summons. But Othello does not boast of it, he just refers to it. Iago had painted the picture of the classical Braggart Soldier, but Othello is not one.

His eloquence, which G. Wilson Knight calls "the Othello Music", becomes known in the next scene. Here while messengers have gone to fetch Desdemona, he answers Brabantio's charge of witchcraft:

> Wherein I spoke of most disastrous chances,
> Of moving accidents by flood and field;
> Of hair-breadth scapes i'th' imminent deadly breach;
> Of being taken by the insolent foe;
> And sold to slavery, and my redemption thence.[15]

This is a long speech, covering more than forty lines, and he holds the senators spell-bound. The Duke says:

> I think such a tale would win my daughter too.[16]

After this episode of trial is over, he is told of the danger to Cyprus and that he will have to leave for Cyprus immediately. This has been sprung upon him all of a sudden, but he is forthwith ready to go.

When we see him again in the next scene he speaks some of the best lines in Shakespeare on his union with Desdemona. It is Othello the lover who is speaking here but Othello the statesman does not forget his duty. He announces the fact that the Turks have been destroyed by the tempest and in the next scene issues a proclamation of revelry to celebrate this victory won without any battle. In scene iii he posts Cassio on guard duty and withdraws. When, roused by the alarm bell, he comes in, he shows himself to be a just and fair-minded person. It is only after listening to an account of the brawl from Iago, who appears to speak most reluctantly, that he dismisses Cassio.

It is in Act iii, scene iii, which is the longest scene in the play that the Temptation starts, Opinions differ on his succumbing to temptation. There are some critics who suggest that the seeds of jealousy had already been dormant in his mind and some who take a more positive view.

> His tragedy lies in this—that whole nature was indisposed to jealousy, and yet was such that he was unusually open to deception.[17]

Apart from these two opposing points of view, a very valuable opinion has been made that succumbing to jealousy and his actions thereafter are not consistent with his character:

> The audience, after seeing how noble a character Othello is, does not expect him to succumb to Iago. He expects Othello to soundly beat up Iago for his insolence it is denied him and the hero can never really recover in his estimation. The first two Acts, by engrossing the spectator so effectively in Othello's life and being, have prepared him for some such response. The onlooker is similarly expectant of Hamlet going on being Hamlet, and Macbeth, Macbeth and he was not disappointed. Nothing they do lets down expectations in this way.[18]

This means that there is a lack of consistency in Othello's character. This critic, John Bayley, however, does not refer to Aristotle in this connection. Consistency is the most important of the four traits described by Aristotle, as has already been mentioned above. The factor of inconsistency as outlined by Bayley depends on one's viewpoints. If one adopts Bradley's viewpoint then there is no inconsistency. Those critics like Leavis also, who believe that the seeds of jealousy were already in Othello, will not find it. Bayley's point of view, however, argues the lack of consistency, which, by Aristotelian standards, would be a serious flow.

The scene in which he faints and falls down (Act IV, scene i) is the lowest point in his career, this is also the eaves-dropping scene, a scene which shows him spying upon Cassio. Spying is ignoble in itself and in this case it is all the more so because he is being made a fool of. The occasion for fainting comes earlier. He is so overcome by jealousy that he speaks in a disjointed manner and faints:

> It is not words that shake me thus.
> Pish! Noses, ears and lips. Is't possible?
> —Confession?—Handkerchief?—O devil!
> (*He falls down*).[19]

The Othello whose eloquence had won him Desdemona has come to this. It is only in the last scene that he will recover his former dignity and eloquence. But before that there are three more occasions to highlight the depth which he has fallen. After the eaves-dropping, in the same scene Lodovico brings him a letter from Venice and Othello strikes Desdemona in front of everyone.

In the next scene, first he spies upon Desdemona by asking Emilia about her, and then there is the sequence known as the Brothel-scene. Here he treats Desdemona as though she were a prostitute. He could not have hit upon anything else to hurt her more.

After this he makes two brief appearances in sc. iii of this Act, and in sc. i of the fifth Act, before the last scene. These appearances are not very important ones.

The last scene opens with the famous speech beginning "'tis the cause". This speech shows that Othello has got his eloquence back. This is his second soliloquy and as Nevill Coghill has observed, the decision to kill Desdemona has already been taken, it is not that he takes it here:

> he has decided upon what to do, and what he says is the embroidery on that decision, not the argument that led him up to it.[20]

The speech has been extensively commented upon, positive as well as negative. A neutral view has been taken by Stanley Cavell:

> the words are those of a man in a trance, in a dream-state, fighting not to awaken, willing for anything but light.[21]

Othello does not want Desdemona to die un-shriven, so he kisses her till she wakes and then tells her to confess her sins, particularly that of adultery. She, being innocent, does not do so, and he strangles her.

Then Emilia comes in to tell him of the attack on Cassio, and, after sometime manages to convince him of Desdemona's innocence. Then there is only one course open to him—that of killing himself and he takes it. Before he commits suicide he delivers another of his famous speeches which again, has been interpreted in various ways, positive as well as negative.

Othello thus is presented as a noble and heroic man who, through jealousy, ruins himself. He thus fulfills the Aristotelian requirements. Except for John Bayley, no one has thought of pointing out inconsistency in his character. From the Aristotelian point of view, his *hamartia* was not jealousy. His error of judgment lay in trusting Iago.

Othello, along with *The Winter's Tale*, has been looked upon as a study in jealousy—how this ignoble emotion demeans and finally destroys a man who is essentially noble. The romance ends happily for King Leontes is given the chance to repent for sixteen years, but *Othello* ends tragically.

There remains one more point to be mentioned—whether Othello was white or a negro. At present, it is generally accepted that he was the latter but earlier that was not the case. Coleridge for example, found it:

> ...somewhat monstrous to conceive this beautiful Venetian girl falling in love with a veritable negro...which Shakespeare does not appear to have in the least contemplated.[22]

Coleridge, later, admits that he, if not a negro, was coloured, a Moor. This is not the modern attitude. Ridley for example is ready to accept him as a noble negro.

> I feel, therefore, that Othello should be imagined in reading, and presented on the stage, as coal-black, a negro.[23]

(c) Iago

Iago is the most unmitigated villain in Shakespeare. Usually Shakespeare gives a touch of softness even to his villains, thus making them credible as human beings, but there is no such touch in Iago.

The best-known critical remark about Iago is that given by Coleridge:

> ...the motive-hunting of motiveless malignity.[24]

Actually however, Iago's malignance is not so very motiveless, at least not to himself. He gives two causes for his "double knavery" in his very first soliloquy: (a) the fact that he has been superseded by Cassio and (b) perhaps Othello has seduced his wife. There is, above everything, his simple statement "I hate the Moor". No reasons are needed for this hatred. Just no reasons are needed for loving a person. There might be scores of reasons, insignificant in themselves, which might lead to hatred or to love.

Iago is present in all the scenes except two—the proclamation scene, in which all the characters are absent, and the willow-scene. In this he goes one better than Othello, for Othello is absent in three. There is another feature in which he gains more prominence than Othello—he has eight soliloquies whereas the latter has only three. (*Vide* Chapter 9 *infra, Certain Elizabethan Features*).

We see him being besieged by Roderigo in the first scene who complains that in spite of lavish expenditure his suit to Desdemona has not prospered. Iago pacifies him. Indeed he pacifies Roderigo throughout the play. He tells Roderigo how he hates Othello for having preferred Cassio to him. He makes his hypocrisy clear in a speech:

> O, Sir, content you.
> I follow him to serve my turn upon him.
> ... ...
> But I will wear my heart upon my sleeve,
> For doves to peck at: I am not what I am.[25]

It is this half-line that expresses the essential Iago: "I am not what I am." Fluchère, with these and other such lines in mind says:

> Iago, indeed, possesses all the traits of the Renaissance villain: he reveals himself openly either by his asides to the audience or in his scenes with Rederigo.[26]

Iago's machiavellianism thus becomes apparent right at the outset. He is, as a matter of fact, the perfect machiavellian villain. His duplicity is even more highlighted when he talks to Othello in the next scene. He pretends to be so loyal as to resent

Brabantio's insulting remarks upon Othello. The Machiavellian villain is a plotter and this aspect becomes clear in his first soliloquy in which he plans to make Othello jealous concerning Cassio.

Another aspect of his duplicity is that he has got himself a reputation for honesty and everyone refers to him as "honest Iago". There are, as Empson has analysed, fifty-two uses of the words "honest" and "honesty" in the play. Most of them refer to him or are used by him.

In the next scene (Act I, scene iii) he speaks only towards the end. Not only does he tell Roderigo that Desdemona will soon tire of Othello, but also reveals his cynicism:

> Virtue! a fig! 'Tis in ourselves, that we are thus, or thus.[27]

After this he persuades Roderigo to follow them to Cyprus. He tells him to take money with him and it is remarkable how many times he says this. For example in the passage beginning with the remark "It is merely a lust of the blood" he says it eight times and in all he says it eleven times.

His first remarks in Cyprus concern the remarkable performance in giving out the impromptu completes for Desdemona's entertainment. The foregoing dialogues are not significant. There are ten couplets here about which Nevill Coghill says:

> ...as elegant as anything in *The Rape of the Lock*. It succeeds completely in taking Desdemona's mind off her worries and shows Iago's amusing social gifts.[28]

Thus another unsuspected aspect of his character is here revealed. The ability to versify was one of the social accomplishments of a gentleman in Elizabethan times.

His machinations start after this. It is remarkable how cleverly he engineers the whole thing. It is not surprising that Wilson Knight should call him a man of intellect, for he sets about his work with cold-blooded detachment and premeditation. All the time he acts as if he is very reluctant, as if Othello is forcing him to say what he does not want to say. This is what M.R. Ridley calls his "usual tactics of exasperating caution".[29]

This begins with the way in which he gets Cassio's dismissal. He engineers the whole thing with Roderigo's help, but nobody suspects this. He pretends to speak most reluctantly against Cassio and this pretence is carried on into the temptation scene. In between come two more of his soliloquies which reveal his intriguing as well as his attitude.

In the temptation scene, his manipulation of Othello is masterly. He starts with an innocent question and goes on giving hints and insinuations so that at the end he has managed to make Othello conscious of his inferiority and also of the fact that Desdemona, since she has deceived her father, may deceive him also. It is in this scene that he gets her handkerchief, which she drops.

As has been observed, fate favours him. Now that he has got the handkerchief, he can easily tell Othello that Desdemona has given it to Cassio, for he plans, in his sixth soliloquy, to plant it in his rooms. By this time Othello is thoroughly jealous and takes his vow. Iago also takes the vow to help him. Thus the two aims of his "double knavery" are achieved, for Othello appoints him his lieutenant in Cassio's place.

In the next scene, Cassio gives Bianca the handkerchief, and the scene after that is the well-known eaves-dropping scene. All coincidences play into Iago's hands, for Bianca, too, comes in with the handkerchief in her hand. It is in this scene that he suggests strangling to Othello. This is the man to whom Desdemona turns for help in the brothel scene.

He behaves towards her with great sympathy and a few minutes after continues his villainy by plotting Cassio's murder with Roderigo.

After this comes the willow-scene in which he does not appear. This is followed by the scene in which Cassio's murder is attempted. We have his last and eighth soliloquy in which he decides that both Cassio and Roderigo have to die. Then in the confusion of darkness he wounds Cassio in the leg and few minutes later enters with a lantern, all innocent helpfulness, and kills Roderigo.

His presence of mind in this scene is wonderful. He takes command of the situation in such a way that Lodovico and Gratiano, who are both present, have no occasion to take offence. He sees to everything. Bianca comes in unexpectedly and he at once seizes the chance to incriminate her. Emilia comes in and at once he sends her to Othello to give him the news.

After this comes the last scene. He comes in, never dreaming that Emilia will betray him. He tries to browbeat her, but she exposes his villainy. He is full of confidence and answers Emilia's charges quite coolly:

> I told him what I thought, and told no more
> Than what he found himself was apt and true.[30]

Othello is present on the stage and Iago thinks he will support him, and so he does till Emilia's revelations about the handkerchief. Then all hope is gone and he stabs Emilia. This shows that there is not a particle of love for her in him. He tries to escape but gets caught. Chances and coincidences had favoured him earlier, but they do not do so any more. He says his last words:

> Demand me nothing, what you know, you know,
> From this time forth I never will speak word.[31]

Proofs of his conspiracy against Cassio are found on the dead body of Roderigo. There are three such papers which incriminate him.

In Iago, Shakespeare has presented the true machiavellian, a man who is a relentless plotter. M.R. Ridley calls him:

> ...not a long-term strategist, but a superbly skilful and opportunist tactician.[32]

He can quickly adjust himself to every circumstance, can turn every event to his own advantage, he has been seen as the epitome of an intellect that has turned to evil. A.C. Bradley had declared that he is the most masterly and the subtlest of Shakespeare's villains:

> Iago stands supreme among Shakespeare's evil characters because the greatest intensity and subtlety of imagination have gone to his making.[33]

He compares Iago with Richard III, with Milton's Satan and Goethe's Mephistopheles and finds Iago superior to all of them. Much the same attitude is prevalent in later criticism also. More than eight decades after Bradley, Anthony Hecht uses words like "fiendishness" with reference to him. As a villain he is incomparable.

(d) Cassio

Many critics have classified Cassio as a minor character. No less an authority than Dr. Johnson has done so. Yet he shall be included within the category of major characters here because much of the action hinges upon him. This feature has been pointed out by M.R. Ridley.

> He is somehow a rather indeterminate figure and it is not altogether easy to see why this is so.... The truth is, I think, that Cassio is primarily a "pivotal" figure, of great importance to the movement of the play, but not of much importance as a person.[34]

Some other modern critics, also, tend to give him more importance than earlier critics did. As a matter of fact, Cassio stands on the border-line between the major and the minor characters and cannot be definitely included as belonging to any one of them. This is the case with many Shakespearean characters, Banquo in *Macbeth* being one.

Cassio may not be an important person according to Ridley, but he is a fully credible human being. He is perhaps the most normal among the chief characters. His character has been summed up by Dr. Johnson:

> Cassio is brave, benevolent and honest, ruined only by his want of stubbornness to resist an insidious invitation.[35]

This summary of his character has been accepted by later critics. As a matter of fact, Iago's summing up of his character is the best. Early in the play he paints a most unfavourable picture of Cassio to Roderigo, but when referring to him in his soliloquy (in which, it can be taken, there is no pretence) he admits:

> He has a daily beauty in his life,
> That makes me ugly.[36]

This is the true homage of villainy to goodness, for, except for the drunken scene, Cassio is everywhere presented as a noble and eminently lovable man.

His attitude towards Othello and Desdemona brings out the best in him. To Othello, his attitude is that of simple hero-worship. It is not that he speaks of Othello, in a rapturous manner as he does about Desdemona, but his high esteem for Othello and his devotion to him is apparent in the few references that he does make to him. His worshipful adoration for Desdemona is far more outspoken:

A maid
That paragons description and wild game:
One that excels the quirks of blazoning pen,
And in the essential vesture of creation
Does bear all excellency.[37]

The capacity for such pure-spirited adoration argues a nobility of the heart that is the very opposite of Iago's cynicism. It is the attitude of Courtly Love.

Apart from this, his main function in the play, of course, lies in his influence on the plot. All unknown to himself, he is the cause of the tragic end of the play. Iago makes shameful use of him (as he does, indeed, of everyone) again and again. First of all he, in the second Act, makes Cassio drunk so as to cause his dismissal. Then he advises him to ask Desdemona to plead for him, then he makes him talk about Bianca in such a way that Othello can think he is talking about Desdemona. Finally he tries to kill Cassio. Cassio is no less a sufferer of Iago's machinations than Othello is. Every time that Iago manipulates him; his influence on the plot becomes apparent. Had he not been there, the tragedy *Othello* would not have existed. It is true that he is a border-line figure between the major characters and the minor ones, but such divisions matter only in a work like the present one. As a dramatic character he is a fully credible, three-dimensional figure, fulfilling all the four Aristotelian requirements most satisfactorily, more so than anyone else.

(e) Desdemona

Dr. Johnson summing up of Desdemona's character is one that the majority of critics agree with, though there are one or two exceptions. He finds Desdemona's character to be an admirable example of Shakespeare's workmanship:

> The soft simplicity of Desdemona, confident of merit and conscious of innocence, her artless perseverance in her suit, and her slowness to suspect that she can be suspected, are such proofs of Shakespeare's skill in human nature, as, I suppose, it is vain to seek in any modern writer.[38]

Desdemona is, indeed, one of the most wonderful creations of Shakespeare. Bradley clearly worships her and so does G. Wilson Knight. Yet there are a few critics who have found her disagreeable. The most outspoken of them is John Quincy Adam, the sixth President of America. He finds Desdemona to be hardly better than "a wanton".

> Her conversation with Emilia indicated unsettled principles even with regard to the obligations of the nuptial tie, and she allows Iago, almost unrebuked, to banter with her very coarsely on women.... When Othello smothers her in bed, the terror and the pity subside immediately into the sentiment that she has her deserts.[39]

Not everyone, however, is as pitiless as this, and the majority of critics agree in finding her a sweet, virtuous, innocent and a pathetic figure.

Not only is she sweet and feminine, but a dignified character. This is the first trait to strike one when she enters in the third scene of the first Act. She says in answer to Brabantio:

> My noble father,
> I do perceive here a divided duty:
> To you I am bound for life and education,
> My life and education both do learn me
> How to respect you, you are lord of all my duty.[40]

Then she goes on to explain her loyalty to her husband. It is a speech of quiet dignity, the speech of an adult, fully responsible woman, belying the criticism which many has made, that she is not an intelligent person. She shows great self-respect after this, when the question of her staying with her father comes up. She chooses to go with her husband, following the drum, rather than stay with Brabantio where she is not wanted.

She has been called "warmly human" and is said to have "a certain domestic femininity" by G. Wilson Knight,[41] which comes out in the scene in which she is pleading for Cassio (Act III, scene iii). But, after this, jealousy transforms Othello and there is the scene about the handkerchief. Even in this scene, with Othello in the ugly mood he is in, she makes a stand for herself.

> Des.: It is not lost, but what an if it were?
> Oth.: Ha!
> Des.: I say it is not lost.
> Oth.: Fetch't, let me see it.
> Des.: Why, so I can sir, but I will not now.
> This is a trick, to put me from my suit.[42]

Here she shows considerable strength of personality to stand up against Othello. She has been thought to be entirely defenceless and passive, but that comes later, when Othello becomes truly violent. Then, indeed, she can do nothing, as in the scene where he strikes her publicly.

Later in the brothel scene, he insults her in an unprecedented manner, but she defends her chastity and her honour:

> Des.: By heaven, you do me wrong.
> Oth.: Are not you a strumpet?
> Des.: No, as I am a Christian
> If to preserve this vessel for my lord
> From any hated foul unlawful touch
> Be not to be a strumpet, I am none.[43]

There is great dignity in her and the pride that true chastity brings. Carol Thomas Neely has highlighted this point:

> Desdemona's spirit, clarity and realism do not desert her entirely in the latter half of the play as many critics and performers imply.[44]

But she is left disconsolate, in tears, so that she turns to Iago for help. Even then, she musters up the energy and courage to attend a public banquet.

The willow scene, coming after this, again shows an entirely feminine, domestic side of her character. This scene is entirely Shakespeare's own. There is nothing like it in Cinthio's story. It gives a picture of domestic peace:

> It is the only calm scene of domestic behaviour...entirely free of role-playing deception.[45]

Here we see a calm friendship between Desdemona and Emilia, and they talk of many things. An ominous note is struck by Desdemona when she says, perhaps in jest (it depends upon the actress):

> If I do die before thee, prithee shroud me
> In one of those same sheets.[46]

She is in a perplexed, as well as sad mood and the lines can be seen as premonitions of disaster. This instance of coming events casting their shadows before can be seen many times in Elizabethan drama. There is no doubt about her sadness, for she says that the tragic fate of her mother's maid is haunting her. This girl was in love with a young man who turned out to be mad and left her. The girl died singing a song:

> She had a song of "willow',
> And she died singing it, that song to-night
> Will not go from my mind.[47]

Haunted by the song, she sings it. It is a sad song, associated with the death of the maid and betrayal by her lover. What is more portentous, it refers, in the last line, to marital infidelity. Then comes a revealing passage of dialogue. Desdemona wants to know if Emilia knows of women who have betrayed their husbands and asks if she would do so "for all the world". Emilia asks her what she herself would do in such a case and Desdemona answers with a strong negative: "No, by this heavenly light." Emilia, taking a very practical stance says that if she had the whole world in exchange, she would betray her husband. Even then Desdemona flatly refuses to believe her:

> I do not think there is any such woman.[48]

This is very significant. It can be taken to mean, (a) she is truly thinking there is no such woman and (b) she cannot bring herself to recognize the ugly fact that such women exist. Whatever it is, it proves that she herself is incapable of being unfaithful to her husband.

When the scene ends, it ends with a Senecan couplet spoken by her that makes her character even clearer:

> God me such usage send,
> Not to pick bad from bad, but by bad mend! [49]

In other words, she prays that God will give her the strength to learn from evil how to overcome it. Her character, in other words, is so pure that she finds it difficult even to contemplate evil, and will only learn to avoid it or to overcome it, not to tolerate it. This scene, more than any other leaves us with a sense of her purity and also the realisation of how little Othello knows her.

In the murder scene she is puzzled and afraid at first and, as Othello reveals the cause of his jealousy, telling her that Cassio has confessed to having committed adultery with her, she loses heart and pleads with him. After he has supposedly killed her she becomes conscious again and recovers her voice enough to protest her innocence. Then, even in that condition, she tries to save Othello by saying that she has killed herself before she finally dies.

Much has been said about this recovery of consciousness as far as stage-craft is concerned (*vide* Chapter 5 *supra*). Here what concerns us is the forgiveness and love she has for Othello. When Emilia asks who has killed her she says:

> Nobody, I myself, farewell:
> Commend me to my kind lord, O, farewell! (she dies).[50]

Such an example of Christian love and forgiveness is impossible to find. Prospero also forgives his enemies, but only after more than a decade of growing self-realisation. Desdemona forgives her poor deluded murderer husband then and there. As Bradley has said:

> She thus becomes at once the most beautiful example of this love and the most pathetic heroine in Shakespeare's world.[51]

The major characters in this play, thus, show great variety. Indeed, each one is unique in himself. Othello is a unique example of a jealous husband for, unlike Leontes in *The Winter's Tale* he is denied the grace of repentance in full and as soon as the realisation of his crime dawns on him, he kills himself. Desdemona is also unique, in her personality as well as her pathetic end. Iago of course, stands absolutely unparalleled among Shakespeare's villains. There are not many characters in *Othello*, but each is unique in his or her sphere.

References

1. Fluchère, *op.cit.*, p. 19.
2. Butcher, S.H., *Aristotle's Theory of Poetry and Fine Art* with a Critical Text translation of *The Poetics*. New Delhi, Kalyani Pubs., 1981, Chapter xv, p. 53.
3. *Ibid.*
4. *Ibid.*, p. 45.
5. *Ibid.*, p. 57.
6. Wain, John, *op.cit.*, pp. 39, 42.
7. *Ibid.*, p. 50.
8. Bradley, A.C., *op.cit.*, pp. 151, 154.
9. Ridley, *op.cit.*, p. xlix.
10. Act I, scene ii, ll. 18-19, p. 16.
11. Bloom, Harold, *op.cit.*, p. 124.
12. Act I, scene ii, l. 59, p. 19.
13. Act I, scene ii, ll. 60-61, p. 19.
14. Act I, scene ii, ll. 87-88, p. 20.
15. Act I, scene iii, ll. 34-38, pp. 28-29.
16. Act I. scene iii, l. 171, p. 31.
17. Bayley, *op.cit.*, p. 151.
18. Bayley, John, *Tragedy and Consciousness: Othello*, in Wain, John, *op.cit.*, pp. 166-67.
19. Act IV, scene i, ll. 14-43, p. 137.
20. Coghill, Nevill, *Shakespeare's Professional Skill*, in Wain, *op. cit.*, p. 152.
21. Cavell, Stanley, *Epistemology and Tragedy: A Reading of Othello*, in Bloom, *op. cit.*, p. 14.
22. Quoted in Ridley, *op. cit.*, p. liii.

23. *Ibid.*
24. Wain, *op. cit.*, p. 53.
25. Act, scene i, ll. 41-42, 64-65, pp. 6-8.
26. Fluchère's *op.cit.*, p. 224.
27. Act I, scene iii, ll. 319-20, p. 40.
28. Wain. *op.cit.*, p. 150.
29. Ridley, *op.cit.*, p. 119.
30. Act V, scene ii, ll. 177-78, p. 187.
31. Act V, scene ii, ll. 304-05, p. 194.
32. Ridley, *op.cit.*, p. lxi.
33. Bradley, *op.cit.*, p. 190.
34. Ridley, *op.cit.*, p. lxv.
35. Wain, *op.cit.*, p. 50.
36. Act V, scene i, ll. 19-20, p. 171.
37. Act II, scene i, ll. 61-65, p. 51.
38. Wain, *op.cit.*, p. 50.
39. *Ibid.*, p. 25.
40. Act I, scene iii, ll. 180-84, p. 31.
41. Knight, *op.cit.*, p. 107.
42. Act III, scene iv, ll. 80-84, p. 128.
43. Act IV, scene ii, ll. 84-87, p. 155.
44. Wain, *op.cit.*, p. 88.
45. *Ibid.*, p. 205.
46. Act IV, scene iii, ll. 24-25, p. 165.
47. Act IV, scene iii, ll. 28-31, p. 165.
48. Act IV, scene iii, l. 83, p. 168.
49. Act IV, scene iii, ll. 104-05, p. 169.
50. Act V, scene ii, ll. 125-26, pp. 184-85.
51. Bradley, *op.cit.*, p. 166.

8

The Minor Characters

There are very few dramatists who play as much attention to their minor characters as Shakespeare does. This, among many others, is one of the reasons for his supremacy over his contemporaries. Even those characters who speak but a few lines are given individuality. His critics have always been alive to this feature, and Dr. Johnson has pointed out with particular reference to *Othello*:

> Even the inferior characters of this play would be very conspicuous in any other piece, not only for their justness but their strength.[1]

Othello is a mature play and, as pointed out by Dr. Johnson, each character, however unimportant he may be, has been endowed, in addition to the two qualities mentioned by Dr. Johnson, with a rounded individuality of his own. In the discussion given below the same order will be followed as has been given in the text. According to this, Brabantio is the first of them.

(a) Brabantio

Brabantio, though as the heroine's father, occupies a significant place on the play, has been neglected by Shakespearean critics, this is perhaps because he is a rather unattractive character, particularly according to modern standards as he is the traditional heavy father, carrying comic associations.

As such, however, he is a fully credible, three-dimensional figure. We see him only in the first three scenes, but in them he plays a major part. Throughout, he behaves exactly as he is expected to behave. He is naturally angry at being rudely summoned in the first scene. At first he is incredulous and on being told about Desdemona's elopement blames Roderigo of creating disturbance for being rejected by him. Then when he finds the allegation to be only too true it is to Roderigo he turns for more information. He admits that he would rather have had him as his son-in-law than Othello. He finds it absolutely unbelievable that Desdemona should fall in love with Othello. For him it is something unnatural, and this he clarifies in the next scene when he accuses Othello of having cast a magic spell over her:

> Thou hast practis'd on her with foul charms,
> Abus'd her delicate youth, with drugs or minerals,
> That weakness motion.[2]

He behaves with great self-confidence in the next scene. He has no doubt that his complaints against Othello will be seriously attended to, and Othello will be punished, for having used witchcraft to captivate Desdemona. He is to be pitted in this instance, for he has no idea how important Othello is to the senators and to the state of Venice. So he accuses Othello.

> Here is the man, this Moor, whom now it seems
> Your special mandate, for the state-affairs,
> Hath hither brought.[3]

After painting a picture of Desdemona as quiet, shy girl, most unlikely to fall in love and elope with a lover she knows would be most unwelcome to her father, he accuses Othello of having used magic to seduce her. When Desdemona enters, he still believes that he has the right perspective on the affair. He addresses her with great confidence:

> Come hither, gentle mistress:
> Do you perceive in all this noble company,
> Where most you owe obedience?[4]

It is only when Desdemona, in a gentle but firm and dignified manner, says that now, at present, she owes obedience to her husband and not to her father that at last he realises that not only has he lost her, but that his accusations against Othello also have become fruitless. He accepts this and behaves with extraordinary dignity, neither blustering, nor becoming pitiful:

> Come hither, Moor:
> I here do give thee that, with all my heart,
> What, but thou hast already, with all my heart
> I would keep from thee. For your sake (jewell)
> I am glad at soul I have no other child,
> For thy escape would teach me tyranny.[5]

He shows himself at his best in this speech. Shakespeare has portrayed, not a mere bad-tempered heavy father, but a dignified man who can adjust himself to circumstances. Herein lies the touch of individualisation that has made Shakespeare an acknowledged master.

After this he speaks a few Senecan couplets following those delivered by the Duke. In these couplets, there is dignified reference to his grief and his broken heart:

> But he bears both the sentence and the sorrow,
> That, to play grief, must of poor patience borrow.
> ... ...
> But words are words; I never yet did hear
> That the bruised heart was pierced through the ear.[6]

Truly, these dignified lines speak of sorrow, but they do not give an inkling of the heartbreak he suffered. We are told about this in the last scene by Gratiano:

> Poor Desdemona, I am glad thy father's dead;
> Thy match was mortal to him, and pure grief
> Shore his old thread atwain.[7]

This, indeed, shows what a fine sense of character, of human nature, Shakespeare had. Brabantio is no mere heavy father who has been betrayed and deserted by his daughter, his only child, in his old age. Such a father is usually a figure of fun in comedies. Instead, we have an intensely individualised figure.

(b) Roderigo

As we have listed Cassio, who comes next to Brabantio in the *Dramatis Personae*, as major character, the next minor character is Roderigo. It should be noted at the very outset that he is an invention of Shakespeare's. There is no such character in Cinthio's story or novella (*vide* Chapter 9 *infra*).

Roderigo is present in seven scenes and speaks almost a thousand lines. He is a young man of fashion, a suitor of Desdemona and a rejected suitor at that. In addition he is a gull, and a foil to Iago. This is highlighted since most of the time the two appear together. In fact, Roderigo does not have a single scene in which he is not conversing with Iago. He is always fooled by Iago, and the final fooling occurs when Iago ruthlessly kills him. G. Wilson Knight sees him mainly as a foil to Iago:

> Roderigo is his natural companion: the fool is a convenient implement and at the same time continual food for his philosophy.[8]

Carol Thomas Neely takes this character very seriously. She does not dismiss him with a few words as a fool, as Wilson Knight does. To her, he is the typical man:

> Roderigo, most obviously a coxcomb, shows in exaggerated fashion the dangerous combination of romanticism and misogyny and the dissociation of love and sex that all the men share.[9]

This is to treat him rather severely. Besides, had he been a true misogynist he would not have been Desdemona's suitor all, let alone follow her to Cyprus in the vain hope that she will look favourably upon him. His misogyny is only a pose, adopted by him because he thinks it is in fashion and Iago is a misogynist. His sincerity about his love for Desdemona is amply in evidence when he realises that there is no hope for him:

> It is silliness to live, when to live is a torment; and then we have a prescription to die, when death is our physician.
>
> ... ...
>
> What should I do? I confess it is my shame to be so fond, but it is not in my virtue to amend it.[10]

This is no vain speech of a coxcomb, but truly that of a broken-hearted lover. But it is true that in allowing himself to be persuaded by Iago again and again he presents a picture of the most complete gull. He has gone on giving money and jewellery to Iago as presents for Desdemona. This is made clear in the opening lines of the play. It should be noted that Roderigo has been accorded the honour of opening the play:

> Tush, never tell me, I take it much unkindly
> That thou, Iago, who hast had my purse,
> As if the strings were thine, shouldst know of this.[11]

He has allowed himself to be bled by Iago and he will continue to do so even after this. Iago easily persuades him to take more money and follow them to Cyprus in the hope that soon Desdemona will get tired of Othello and be ripe for a lover.

Then in Cyprus Iago persuades him to pick a quarrel with Cassio so as to gain his dismissal. He obediently does so, never dreaming that he is, but a pawn in the hands of the master player. By this time he has spent almost all his money and gets beaten by Cassio in the bargain. But he becomes pacified as soon as Iago points out to him that, in return for it, he has secured the dismissal of Cassio. Dr. Johnson, as usual, shows great interest in the continued credulity of Roderigo and gives it a moral interpretation:

> Roderigo's suspicious credulity and impatient submission to the cheats which he sees practiced upon him and which by persuasion he suffers to be repeated, exhibit a strong picture of a weak mind betrayed by unlawful desires.[12]

Dr. Johnson is severe on the hapless young man for his "unlawful desires", but he has been in love with Desdemona from before her marriage. If he cannot stop loving her now one should not be too severe on him. Indeed he has a romantic, idealistic love for Desdemona, much as Othello himself has. When Iago speaks disparagingly of her he says:

> I cannot believe that in her, she's full of most blest condition.[13]

Apart from this common point between him and Othello, Roderigo serves another important dramatic purpose: he helps in expounding Iago's character. It is in his dialogues with Roderigo that Iago exposes himself the most. It can be said that though he presents hypocritical solutions and advices to

Roderigo, he reveals his character the most to him. His cynicisms, his greed, his machinations, all are exhibited in his dialogues with Roderigo. It shows Shakespeare's wonderful acumen in having invented this character to expose Iago's character in its tortuous details.

He pays, most painfully, for having trusted Iago. Cassio had wounded him in the darkness in the first scene of the fifth Act but he was still alive when Iago entered the stage, then, quick as a flash, Iago stabbed him. Roderigo had hardly any time to realise his villainy:

> O damn'd Iago, O inhuman dog...oh, oh, oh.[14]

No one even hears his piteous cry. Thus he pays for his gullibility and his readiness to ruin Cassio, who had actually done him no harm.

He is significant mainly in that he serves to reveal Iago's character. He also helps to take the plot forward step by step by following Iago's directions. He may be a coxcomb, a gull, a fool, but he is a highly functional character. It is him whom Iago uses to manipulate the events of the plot.

(c) The Duke

The Duke, though he occupies the highest position in the state of Venice, is yet a minor character in the play. He appears in only one scene, the last scene of the first Act and plays an important part in it.

He has called an emergency meeting of the Senate in order to discuss the problem of the Turkish attack on Cyprus and to decide what is to be done about it. He has already sent an urgent summons to Othello, so it is right to suppose that he is thinking of sending him to Cyprus to quell the attack. But before he can take any steps in this direction, he is confronted by Brabantio and his complaints. He shows himself a man of quick decisions and considerable ability to deal with unexpected situations. He knows that he has to depend on Othello for the Turkish attack and can make out that Brabantio's complaint, in any case, cannot be satisfactorily dealt with as Othello and Desdemona have already got married. So he gives sensible advice to Brabantio, to accept all that has happened with good grace, since it cannot be helped. Desdemona's attitude justifies this advice. So he delivers his Senecan couplets:

> When remedies are past, the griefs are ended,
> By seeing the worst, what late on hopes depended.
> To mourn a mischief that is past and gone,
> Is the next way to draw more mischief on.[15]

There are two more couplets to this tune, giving sage advice to Brabantio and then he turns to the real business of the meeting.

Here, no less than in the foregoing matters, he shows himself to be a man of few words and those relevant to the matter at hand. He quickly acquaints Othello with the available facts and tells him that the defence of Cyprus is entrusted to him because he knows the fortifications of the place. As soon as the matter of Desdemona accompanying Othello is settled, he tells the latter to meet him at ten o'clock in the morning and that he must leave an officer behind him so that messages can be sent from Venice.

The Duke is thus portrayed as a sensible and able statesman. He is able to handle a tricky situation in such a way as to cause offence to none and at the same time get his own work done. He serves the useful purpose of shifting the location of the play from Venice to Cyprus and leaves the impression of a strong and tactful statesman.

(d) Montano

Montano has been described in the list of the *Dramatis Personae* as "Othello's predecessor in the government of Cyprus". In other words, he had been occupying a highly responsible post till Othello came. We see him first in the first scene of the second Act.

It can easily be thought that as Montano is being replaced by Othello he will be resentful of the fact and be envious of and hostile to Othello. This, however, is not the case. There is no such thought in his mind. He has come to the quay at Cyprus in order to find out what has happened to the Turkish ships during the terrible storm that has recently raged in and around Cyprus.

Soon enough he receives the good news that the Turkish fleet has been destroyed, so there is no danger to Cyprus any longer. The same messenger gives him the news that Cassio's ship has reached there, and that Othello will be arriving shortly. Montano speaks approvingly of Othello:

> I am gland on 't, 'tis a worthy governor.
> ... ...
> For I have serv'd him, and the man commands
> Like a full soldier.[16]

This makes it clear that there is no resentment in him. He appreciates the abilities of Othello as a soldier. It is he who, with a brief question, elicits from Cassio his worshipful description of Desdemona. Thus he serves the purpose of making us acquainted with Cassio's attitude towards her. He does not say anything more in this scene.

We see him next in the third scene, the drinking scene. Here he shows himself as a worthy boon-companion to Cassio and Iago, joining them good-humouredly in drinking and merrymaking.

Then when Cassio becomes drunk he asks Iago if it is a common practice with him. On being told by Iago that Cassio is a confirmed drunkard, he is shocked and says Othello must be told about this. This is but natural, for he himself has been in a responsible post and knows that man must have dependable assistants. There is no spite against Cassio in this remark.

Then he is assaulted by Cassio and complains against him to Othello in a very restrained manner. After this, the plot is devoted to the main characters and we see Montano only in the last scene.

Emilia cries out for help after Desdemona's death and Montano comes in with Gratiano, Iago and others. After Iago stabs Emilia he quickly takes command of the situation, telling the others to guard the door while he goes out with Gratiano after Iago. After this, though he enters again, he does not speak.

He, thus, is not an important character but Shakespeare has individualised him as a dutiful, good-natured man who can take a position of command if necessary.

(e) Gratiano

Gratiano, the brother of Brabantio is also a character who has been given a definite personality by the dramatist. It is surprising that he enters only in the last Act. Whether he is there with Brabantio in the first Act we do not know, for he is not mentioned. Then when the delegation comes from Venice in Act IV, scene i, only Lodovico is seen on the stage. In the opening part of the willow scene, when the supper has just been concluded. Again Lodovico is on the stage but Gratiano's name is not given. But it is sensible to conclude that he must have come along with Lodovico as a member of the delegation in the fourth Act.

He is brought on the stage, along with Lodovico in the first scene of the fifth Act just after Cassio has wounded Roderigo, and is himself wounded in the leg in the darkness by Iago. Both Lodovico and Gratiano stand overwhelmed and almost inactive while Iago holds the stage, bustling about being efficient. It is he who is holding the only lantern, so he can do very much as he likes, pretending to look after Cassio, killing Roderigo, catching Bianca and all the rest of it. Lodovico and Gratiano stand buzzed, not knowing what to do. Gratiano, like Lodovico, speaks just a few lines here and there in this scene.

It is when he comes in the last scene with Montano that he speaks a few lines. The most important of them is the passage about Brabantio's death. He thus, serves the useful purpose of acquainting the audience with this fact:

> Poor Desdemona, I am glad thy father's dead
> Thy match was mortal to him, and pure grief
> Shore his old thread atwain: did he live now
> This sight would make him do a desperate turn,
> Yea, curse his better angel from his side
> And fall to reprobation.[17]

This is his longest speech and with it his function in the play becomes clear. After this he only speaks one or two lines as the other characters do.

It cannot be denied that Shakespeare has been a bit negligent with him. It is true that he serves the purpose of telling us about Brabantio's death, but that is the only thing he does. Shakespeare does not give his name in the scenes in which he is likely to be present nor does he tell us when the time he arrives at Cyprus.

(f) Lodovico

Lodovico has been given more importance than Gratiano, though he is designated as but a "kinsman of Brabantio" and Gratiano is his brother. Thus Lodovico is Desdemona's cousin whereas Gratiano is her uncle. So according to the degree of relationship, Gratiano is more important. As a dramatic character, however, Lodovico is given more importance.

He enters the stage for the first time in Act IV, scene i, as a Venetian delegate, bearing an important message for Othello. This letter recalls Othello to Venice, appointing Cassio as governor in his place. While Othello is reading the letter Lodovico talks to Desdemona and Iago and comes to know about Cassio's disgrace. Othello, listening in on this conversation, is inflamed by jealousy and Lodovico, not knowing the true cause, thinks he is angry at his recall to Venice. Then Othello behaves in an unforgivable manner, he strikes Desdemona. Lodovico is shocked and rebukes him:

> My lord, this would not be believ'd in Venice,
> Though I should swear I saw't: 'tie very much,
> Make her amends, she weeps.[18]

After Othello has left Lodovico expresses his incredulous surprise at the change in Othello. He himself is a cultured, sophisticated aristocrat. The savagery of Othello is beyond the limits of civilised behaviour. So he wonders whether Othello is sane or not:

> Is this the noble Moor, whom our full senate
> Call all in all sufficient?
> ... ...
> Are his wits safe? Is he not light of brain? [19]

Iago of course fans the fire in a most deceptive manner and Lodovico is left with the impression that Othello is not as polished a person as he had seemed to be, that at bottom he is quite savage.

In the willow-scene he just says a few lines when leaving after supper. His next important appearance is in the fight scene (V, i). Here he enters with Gratiano, on hearing the outcry made by Cassio and Roderigo. Both of them are confused in the darkness. Lodovico on hearing their cry rightly guesses that more than one person is concerned. He is also apprehensive that the whole thing may be a trap and more help should be got before they investigate the matter.

Then Iago enters with lights and without seeming to, takes command of the situation. Lodovico and Gratiano serve just as props for his activities. His next appearance is in the last scene, along with Montano, Cassio, and Iago as a prisoner. This is the first time he is coming in this scene and is thunderstruck at the turn of events. He easily assumes command in this scene, telling others what to do and addresses Othello:

> O thou Othello, that wert once so good,
> Fall'n in the practice of a damned slave,
> What should be said to thee?[20]

It is he who, after Emilia, unmasks Iago's villainy for he produces letters found in the pockets of Roderigo, both revealing the machiavellian plottings into which Iago has enmeshed Roderigo. After explaining this, he tells Othello that he is hereby divested of his powers and is put under arrest. Cassio is to take up the post that he occupied. Moreover, after Othello has killed himself it is he who delivers the last speech, dispensing justice and restoring order and security in Cyprus. He tells Gratiano to take possession of Othello's property, for he is the rightful heir, and addressing Cassio as Lord Governor, entrusts to him the task of punishing Iago. As is usual, he brings his concluding speech to an end with a Senecan couplet, outlining his future action:

> ...to you, lord governor,
> Remains the censure of this hellish villain,
> The time, the place, the torture: O, enforce it!
> Myself will straight aboard, and to the state
> This heavy act with heavy heart relate.[21]

He is thus a self-possessed, polished aristocrat, able to take command when necessary. He plays the important part of being the emissary from Venice and of concluding the play. As he is Desdemona's cousin, this function he is going to fulfill of telling the state of her death is apt.

(g) Emilia

Emilia is one of the most important minor characters in the play. Carol Thomas Neely, indeed, gives her great importance. According to her, the play's central theme is marital love and conflict between men and women, and she says Emilia is a crucial figure from this point of view as well as in herself:

> It is Emilia who most explicitly speaks to this theme, recognizes this central conflict and inherits from the heroines of comedies, the role of potential mediator of it. She is dramatically and symbolically the play's fulcrum.[22]

Other critics do not accord her this kind of importance, but almost all of them praise her for her loyalty to Desdemona. Rymer, who denigrates every aspect of the play, calls her "who denigrates every aspect of the play", calls her "the meanest woman in the play".[23] Dr. Johnson, as usual, provides much the sanest view:

> ...the virtue of Aemilia is such as we often find worn loosely, but not cost off, easy to commit small crimes, but quickened and alarmed at atrocious villainy.[24]

She enters the stage first with Desdemona, Iago and Roderigo in Act II, scene i, as Desdemona's companion and maid-in-waiting. She speaks very little in this scene (three lines only) which is but proper, as she is in the capacity of something like a servant to Desdemona.

We see her next in Act III, scene I, when she comes to tell Cassio that Desdemona is trying her best to get him reinstated. This is one of those rare occasions when she is alone, that is, not accompanying Desdemona. She then takes Cassio in to meet her mistress and we see this meeting in Act III, scene iii which is the longest scene in the play. She speaks very little in the first part of the scene. This scene is divisible into five sections (*vide*

Chapter 5 *supra*) and it is in the fourth section that she plays, all unawares, a crucial part.

It is in this part of the scene that Desdemona drops her all-important handkerchief and Emilia picks it up, meaning to give it to her husband. She does not know why Iago wants it, but he has asked her many times to get it. She is not betraying Desdemona in picking it up and giving it to Iago, for she has no idea of what use he will put it to:

> What he'll do with it
> Heaven knows, not I,
> I nothing know, but for his fantasy.[25]

As it happens, Iago enters directly and as soon as he comes to know about the handkerchief, snatches it from her. She asks him what he will do with it and tells him to give it back if it is not important. Much has been said about this episode. Rymer, of course, castigates her, but the prevailing opinion is that she is not disloyal to Desdemona. It is difficult to defend her when in the next scene she tells Desdemona that she knows nothing about the handkerchief, but then, as she has already given it to Iago she has nothing else to say. Besides it must be remembered that had she told Desdemona the truth, then the play itself, the tragedy itself, would not have existed, for as soon as Othello asks for it, Desdemona would have told him that Iago had got it.

It is just after this that Othello enters and the gruelling handkerchief scene takes place. Emilia hears the entire dialogue but she never says that she has given the handkerchief to Iago. As has just now been pointed out the tragic plot would have been ruined had she done so. This, however is not a point that critics take account of. A.C. Bradley for example says:

> We know that Othello's jealousy was intimately concerned with the loss of the handkerchief. Emilia, however, certainly failed to perceive this.... In fact, she never thought of it, although she guessed that Othello was being deceived by some scoundrel.... Her stupidity in this matter is gross, but it is stupidity and nothing more.[26]

It is extremely surprising that Bradley does not mention the needs of the plot, which depends upon the secret of Iago's having got the handkerchief from Emilia not being known, not even till the last moment, but after the last moment, that is, after the murder Carol Thomas Neely, however, has pointed out in an oblique manner:

> Emilia, stealing the handkerchief, is catalyst for the play's crisis; revealing its theft, she is catalyst for the play's denouement.[27]

The willow-scene reveals her character more in detail. She takes a practical, rather coarse, woman's point of view of the world of men and women. It is a fully domestic scene with Emilia making Desdemona ready for bed—brushing her hair, etc. and they talk. The importance of this scene has been highlighted by Anthony Brennan. It is a scene which, by showing us the friendliness and affection between the two women, prepares us for Emilia's vindication of Desdemona's character later and her incrimination of her husband. The scene between them, significantly, is longer than any between Othello and Desdemona, covering as it does almost a hundred lines:

> The affection displayed between the women here prepare us for Emilia's loyalty when she returns to the bedchamber later.[28]

Desdemona is so pure-minded that she cannot believe that any woman would deceive her husband. Emilia, acting as a foil to her, replies that she herself would do so if the recompense was worth it. When Desdemona still insists that there are no such women, Emilia delivers her longest speech in the play, a speech of twenty lines. No other minor character has been given such a long speech. Brabantio's speech of accusation is the nearest to it, containing in all eleven full lines and two half-lines, making twelve in all. It is a very revealing speech containing several questions which are actually rhetorical questions, but she answers them. This part is about the infidelity of men. Then she talks about women:

> ...and have not we affections?
> Desire for sport? and frailty, as men have?
> Then let them use us well: else let them know,
> The ills we do, their ills instruct us so.[29]

These and the foregoing lines, while understandably favourable to a feminist interpretation, all the same present a rather cynical picture of married life. As Brennan observes:

> All of her jests about disloyalty to husbands correspond to the picture of Venetian wiles that Iago has shown to Othello.[30]

It is noticeable that Desdemona has no answer to what Emilia says. Perhaps she realises that Emilia's attitude is such that she will not be able to cure her of it, or, herself understand it. This entire dialogue, one of the most famous in the play, serves to contrast and highlight the two women's attitude to marital infidelity.

After this we see Emilia in the murder scene. Bradley's reaction cannot be improved upon:

> Till close to the end she frequently sets one's teeth on edge; and at the end one is ready to worship her.[31]

It will not be an exaggeration to say that she gives her life for her mistress. She achieves a quality usually reserved for the protagonist: tragic pathos. It cannot be said that she has the tragic dignity that inspires pity and terror in the audience, but she definitely has pathos. She attains heroism in defying both Othello and Iago, the only person in the play to do so. More than half a century after Bradley, M.R. Ridley says:

In all the play there is nothing more characteristic of Shakespeare than the way in which Desdemona's death kindles in her a bright flame of self-forgetful courage; it is not just that she faces the threats of both Othello and her husband, but rather that she neglects them, brushes them aside as irrelevant trivialities.[32]

(h) Bianca

Bianca is the third female character in Othello and has been designated as "a Courtesan". M.R. Ridley, referring to this, says:

> I have retained F.'s description of Bianca, since the usual "Mistress to Cassio" implies a more permanent relationship than is anywhere implied in the text.[33]

She has been described by Iago as a woman of easy virtue, not a professional courtesan:

> A housewife that by selling her desires
> Buys herself bread and clothes: it is a creature
> that dotes on Cassio.[34]

As has been explained by Ridley the word "housewife" does not have any pejorative meaning.

> There is also little doubt that Bianca is also a housewife in the normal sense, a citizen of Cyprus, with her own house, and not a mere camp-follower.[35]

She makes her entrance in the fourth scene of the third Act, coming in to greet Cassio, and blames him for not having met her for seven days. Cassio tries to pacify her, and in order to do so, gives her Desdemona's handkerchief which he has found in his room where Iago, unknown to him, had left it. As soon as Bianca sees it, she recognizes it for a typical lover's gift and is jealous. But Cassio soon allays her suspicions:

> I found it in my chamber;
> I like the work well: ere it be demanded.
> As like enough it will, I'ld have it copied.[36]

Then he asks her to leave him as he is going to see Othello. She leaves him after extracting a promise from him that he will meet her.

Except for the fact that Iago says she loves Cassio, this scene gives other indications of her love. The way she accuses Cassio of not having met her, counting the days and hours, might have been said in jest, since she is a courtesan. There is the fact, however, that she becomes jealous on seeing the handkerchief, and pleads with Cassio to see her. All in all, the scene gives the impression that she is in love with Cassio.

After this in the next scene in which Iago describes Bianca (quoted above) there comes the famous eaves-dropping scene in which Cassio talks about Bianca and Othello thinks he is talking about Desdemona. What Cassio says here in answer to Iago's questions, supports the view that Bianca loves him:

> Alas, poor rogue, I think i'faith she loves me.
> She haunts me in every place. I was t'other day

> Talking on the sea-bank, with certain venations
> And thither comes this bauble; by this hand,
> She falls thus about my neck.[37]

After from the fact that this inflames Othello, it is further evidence that Bianca though a courtesan, does really love Cassio. Carol Thomas Neely calls it "Bianca's active open-eyed enduring affection".[38] This critic takes a very positive view.

Then in the course of the scene Bianca herself comes in. She is in a rare temper for she is convinced that the handkerchief is a love token given to Cassio by some woman. She delivers a tirade to that effect, throws the handkerchief to him, flings out a derisive invitation for supper and flounces out. This entrance and exit is extremely important from the dramatic point of view, for it clinches matters for Othello, as he sees the handkerchief in Bianca's hands. But, besides serving this extremely important purpose, it is quite in character and does not seem at all unnatural. Bianca has already shown that she is capable of jealousy and yet wants Cassio. Here the same features are highlighted.

The extent of her love is seen in the fighting scene. Cassio has just left Bianca's house after supper. There is a fight between him and Roderigo and both of them cry out. Hearing their cry some of the characters come out and so does Bianca. Perhaps she had recognized Cassio's voice. What is important is the genuine grief and love she shows on seeing Cassio wounded:

> O my dear Cassio, O my sweet Cassio!
> Cassio, Cassio!
> ... ...
> Alas, he faints! O Cassio, Cassio, Cassio! [39]

She admits, on being questioned by Iago, that Cassio had had supper with her, but she is not afraid, defying the browbeating and vilifications of Iago and Emilia. One admires her genuine devotion to Cassio. Carol Thomas Neely remarks:

> We see her brave the confusion of the night and the ugliness of Iago's insinuations to come to Cassio's side when he is wounded.[40]

This is her last appearance in the play. She appears only three times in the play but leaves a distinct impression of her personality. She may be a woman of easy virtue but her love for Cassio is genuine. She even defies Emilia:

> I am no strumpet, but of life as honest
> As you, that thus abuse me.[41]

One feels that at bottom there is not much difference between the two women. Emilia had not shown herself as extremely virtuous in the willow scene. She had shown herself ready to betray her husband and have love-affairs. Yet she, like a typical woman, abuses one less fortunately placed in life.

Besides these, there are some more characters who come in only for a very short time like the sailors who bring in the news from Cyprus. The messenger bringing the news of the Turkish fleet, the gentleman announcing Othello's proclamation in Act II, scene ii, the Clown in Act III, scene iv and some others. They are too insignificant to be considered separately. What has to be remembered is that Shakespeare gives a definite personality even to his minor creations and this is one of the reasons for his greatness.

References

1. Wain, *op.cit.*, p. 50.
2. Act I, scene ii, ll. 73-75, p. 19.
3. Act I, scene iii, ll. 71-73, p. 25.
4. Act I, scene iii, ll. 178-80, p. 31.
5. Act I, scene iii, ll. 193-97, p. 32.
6. Act I, scene iii, ll. 214-15, 218-19, p. 32.
7. Act V, scene ii, ll. 205-07, 218-19, p. 33.
8. Knight, G.W., *op.cit.*, p. 111.
9. Wain, *op.cit.*, p. 84.
10. Act I, scene iii, ll. 308-18, pp. 39-40.
11. Act I, scene i, ll. 1-3, p. 3.
12. Wain, *op.cit.*, pp. 50-51.
13. Act II, scene i, ll. 247-48, p. 64.
14. Act V, scene i, l. 62, p. 173.
15. Act I, scene iii, ll. 202-05, p. 32.

16. Act II, scene i, ll. 30, 35-36, p. 49.
17. Act V, scene ii, ll. 205-10, p. 188.
18. Act IV, scene i, ll. 236-39, p. 148.
19. Act IV, scene i, ll. 260-61, 265, p. 149.
20. Act V, scene ii, ll. 292-94, p. 193.
21. Act V, scene ii, ll. 368-72, p. 197.
22. Bloom, *op.cit.*, p. 81.
23. Wain, *op.cit.*, p. 48.
24. *Ibid.*, p. 51.
25. Act iii, scene ii, ll. 301-03, p. 111.
26. Bradley, *op.cit.*, p. 196.
27. Wain, *op.cit.*, p. 101.
28. *Ibid.*, p. 205.
29. Act IV, scene iii, ll. 100-03, p. 169.
30. Brennan, Anthony, *Iago, the Strategist of Separation*, in Wain, *op.cit.*, p. 205.
31. Bradley, *op.cit.*, p. 196.
32. Ridley, *op.cit.*, pp. lxvi.
33. *Ibid.*, p. 2 (*N.B.* F. here means the First Folia, printed in 1623).
34. Act IV, scene i, ll. 94-96, p. 141.
35. Ridley, p. 141, fn.
36. Act III, scene iv, ll. 186-88, p. 133.
37. Act IV, scene i, ll. 111, 130-34, p. 143.
38. Bloom, *op.cit.*, p. 87.
39. Act V, scene i, ll. 76, 84, p. 174.
40. Bloom, *op.cit.*, p. 93.
41. Act V, scene i, ll. 121-22.

9

The Plot-structure

At the very beginning of his discussion of Plot Aristotle says:

> The Plot, then, is the first principle, and, as it were, the soul of a tragedy.[1]

He lists it as the first of the six elements of tragedy. He had discussed this element in nine of the twenty-six chapters of *The Poetics*, that is, one-third of the book, laying down many rules. The Elizabethans were fully conversant with them, and followed, or tried to follow them in practice. Some of the basic rules of tragic plot shall now be explained, together with some of the features added on by the Elizabethan.

(a) The Classical Rules, and *Othello*

Let us, at the very outset, have a look at Aristotle's definition of tragedy:

> Tragedy, then, is an imitation of an action that is serious, complete, and of a given magnitude; in language embellished with each kind of artistic ornament, the several kinds being found in separate parts of the play; in the form of action, not of narration; through pity and fear effecting the proper purgation of these emotions.[2]

This definition has many complexities into which it is not possible to go at the moment. However the Elizabethan dramatists treated it as a point of reference, for the rules that follow and the features that shall now be mentioned all follow from it.

The most well-known of the rules are those of the unities. There are three of them: (a) the unity of Action, (b) the unity of Time and (c) the unity of Place. It is a well-known fact that

Shakespeare did not take these rules very seriously, and did not scrupulously observe them except in *The Tempest*. It has been pointed out by M.R. Ridley that *Othello* comes next to *The Tempest* in this respect:

> *Othello* comes much nearer than any of Shakespeare's other great plays except *The Tempest* to observing the unities.[3]

(a) *The Unity of Action*: This is the most important of the rules and refers directly to the definition given above. Aristotle has laid stress on the fact that the action of a tragedy is "serious", which means that there should be no mingling of serious and trivial actions. This rule is specially applicable to tragedies for pity and terror which are the emotions roused by serious action. Shakespeare does not observe this rule for in his tragedies there are frequent comic scenes. There are two scenes in *Othello* in which there are dialogues with a Clown. The drinking scene also provides merrymaking and innocent mirth in the beginning.

(b) *The Unity of Time*: Aristotle allows one full day, "a single revolution of the sun" for the completion of the action of a play. This is quite difficult, but it had been done by Ben Jonson.

As far as Shakespeare is concerned, it is not possible to observe this rule in the Chronicle plays, since such plays spread over a long span of time. As far as *Othello* goes, the time scheme is quite complex.

The main action takes place in Cyprus and this occupies a little less than thirty-six hours. But it is not as simple as this, for is the theory of "double time scheme". This had been pointed out in the middle of the nineteenth century and puts forward the theory of there being two different time-schemes. Act I occupies almost the same time as might be taken in performance. The movement is very rapid:

> The rapid movement of the first
> Act...sets the tempo for the rest of the play.[4]

After this there is quite a long interval between Act I and Act II, definitely a few weeks. Cassio talks of one week, but it must be remembered that the ships did not start out at the same time. There were at least three ships, one with Othello in it, another for Cassio and another for Desdemona. Iago and Roderigo. All this must have taken more than a week.

Once they reach Cyprus, the rest of the play should take place within thirty-six hours. Here it is that the trouble with time starts, for there are repeated references to a longer span of time than mentioned elsewhere. Thus by the time they have landed it is about four o'clock on Saturday for the proclamation is issued at five o'clock. Cassio's dismissal occurs at about ten, for they are just going to resume their duties ("To the platform, masters. Come let's set the watch"[5]). The rest of the action lasts till early Sunday morning. There are several references to the time in the scenes like the one given above.

This is one aspect of the time covered by the action. Yet there is another, a different time scheme that gives the impression of the passing of a far longer span of time, several months at least. For example, according to the scheme given above, after Othello's arrival, Lodovico comes with the letter of recall the very next day. This is impossible, for there had not been enough time for the senators to have received the news about the destruction of the Turkish fleet. Then, throughout the play there are continuous references to a longer interval of time. For example, Bianca accuses Cassio of not having met her for a week. Then, just before the commencement of the eavesdropping scene Iago tells Othello:

> I will make him tell he take anew,
> Where, how, how often, how long ago, and when,
> He has, and is again to cope your wife.[6]

This will naturally mean that the supposed affair between Cassio and Desdemona is a long-standing one. In other words, much more time has elapsed after their reaching Cyprus. Cassio could not have started the affair while crossing the seas, because he came on a different ship. Moreover, it cannot be said that Iago is referring to a pre-marital love-affair because, again and again, the word used is "adultery", implying marriage.

There are, as a matter of fact, thirteen references to time from Act II onwards, all of which suggest that Desdemona's adultery has been going on for quite an appreciable time.

This is one of the peculiarities of the time-scheme of *Othello*, though, as has been pointed out above, the actual action in Cyprus takes about thirty-six hours. There is no flagrant violation of the unity of time. This much of liberty used to be taken by the Elizabethans.

(c) *The Unity of Place*: This implies that all the action should take place in one place only. It should be kept in mind, however, that this was not a rule specifically recommended by Aristotle. It was the writings of the Italian Renaissance, by Scaliger, Minturno, Castelvetro *et al.* that was responsible for this rule. As it was understood by the Elizabethans to mean that there should be no changes of scenes, it was very difficult to follow. The only dramatist who follows it is Ben Jonson, and even he allows himself considerable latitude. Shakespeare did not follow it in *Othello*, for, first of all, there is the shift from Venice to Cyprus. Even in Venice, the two Acts take place in different locations: the first in front of Brabantio's house and the second in the Senate.

When the play shifts to Cyprus, there too the scenes change frequently. They take in the Quay, the Castle, the place in front of the Castle and several rooms within it. The neo-classical critics of his own time and of later times had condemned Shakespeare for not observing these rules. One of the greatest neo-classical critics, Dr. Johnson however, had exonerated him. His defence of the violation of this rule has become famous.

Many other rules, in addition to these, had been laid down by Aristotle. These were later expounded by other critics. Donatus's treatise on drama was one such work. He has explained Aristotle's theory in detail and also added his own. According to him the first section of the play is prologue. This is usually a short speech of coming before the actual action. Marlowe's prologue to *Dr. Faustus* is a very good example of a prologue in the classical manner. Shakespeare too has written prologues to a few of his plays, but usually he incorporates them within the first scene of the play. In *Othello* also this is the case. M.R. Ridley regards the entire first Act as the prologue, for then act II onwards will come the main action and as such

Othello will become a tight-knit play as far as the unities are concerned. In taking this view of the play, he is but following Dr. Johnson who had said:

> Had the scene opened in Cyprus, and the proceeding incidents been occasionally related, there had been little wanting to a drama of the most exact and scrupulous regularity.[7]

Certain other features also have to be observed in writing a tragedy. *Peripeteia* or the Reversal of fortune is one of them. It implies the fall of the hero from a high into a low status. This is clarified by Aristotle. Seeking to explain the ideal plot for a tragedy, he rejects three outlines and finally fixes on the plot that gives a rather good man falling from prosperity into adversity. Othello, too, follows the same pattern. Here we see at first the noble, valiant Moor on whom the state of Venice depends in times of crisis. Then we see his gradual downfall till he kills his innocent wife and himself.

Another important part of the tragic plot is *Anagnorisis* or Recognition. This at its crudest level, involves the mutual recognition of two characters who have been separated, as happens in *Twelfth Night* when Viola and Sebastian recognize each other. The most subtle recognition is that which occurs when a character recognizes his own nature. There are no notable examples of this feature in *Othello* unless Iago's repeated references to his own duplicity are counted as such.

Another important part of the plot, listed by Aristotle after *Peripeteia* and *Anagnorisis,* is *Pathos* or the scene of suffering. This comprises death, physical pain, etc. all tragedies must, of necessity contain such scenes. In *Othello*, in addition to the murder scene, there is the scene in which he strikes her (Act IV, scene i). Apart from physical suffering, there is mental suffering also, and the brothel scene (Act IV, scene ii) can also be included. Moreover, if the sufferings of Othello are to be seriously considered, then the scene of his fainting (Act IV, scene i) should also be included within this category. His sufferings are undoubtedly intense, and they reach a climax when, uttering disjointed words, he loses consciousness in this scene.

(b) Certain Elizabethan Features

The Aristotelian rules take it for granted that a tragedy should have but one plot. Intrigues are expected, but a full-blown sub-plot goes against the rules. They are permitted in comedies, particularly in the New Comedy, but not in tragedies. Elizabethan tragedies, however, often have more than one plot. Usually the sub-plot is a comic one and thus violates the unity of action. Multiplicity of plots is a notable feature of Elizabethan plays, as also is the adoption of disguises. Both of these, however, can be omitted from this discussion as they do not occur in *Othello*.

The soliloquy is an important feature of Elizabethan plays. They are speeches delivered by a character when he is alone on the stage. They deal with the speaker's thoughts. The character may tell us what he is going to do in future; he may tell us about his impression of events that have happened, etc. They are like talking aloud. So far as this aspect of Elizabethan play is concerned *Othello* presents an extraordinary feature. In this play, it is the villain who has got the lion's share of soliloquies; Iago has eight soliloquies whereas Othello has but three. The reasons for this is obvious. Just as Hamlet needs so many soliloquies to express the state of his mind, so Iago needs to express his villainy and his motives for it. In this Iago goes, literally, one better over Hamlet, for Hamlet has seven soliloquies and Iago, eight. Iago's soliloquies have been taken very seriously by Nevill Coghill:

> Iago needs this number to reveal, first, the quality of his own tortuous nature and secondly the detail of his intentions.[8]

Coghill goes on to classify his soliloquies, calling the first three of them "epiphanies" and the last five "signposts".

The first three soliloquies reveal his nature, the working of his mind. All his grudges, his disappointments, his envy, his cynicism, are expressed in them. In this sense, they can be called epiphanies. There is the element of self-deception in them as well, in that he thinks Othello has had an affair with his wife.

This is not supported by anything else or anybody else in the play. It is a figment of his own imagination. He wants to believe it, in order to justify his hatred.

Moreover, Coghill has pointed out that there is a definite development in his villainy in the order in which the first three soliloquies are delivered;

> His first three soliloquies *are graded in heinousness*, the foulest last.[9]

As the soliloquies proceed, the reader or the audience comes to dislike him more and more. This is the extraordinary quality about Iago's soliloquies, for usually soliloquies create sympathy for the speaker as the audience comes to understand him. Here, however, it is the opposite that happens. As it is, Shakespeare has given us a new kind of soliloquy—one that alienates the speaker from the audience. This is perfectly understandable, as Iago is the villain. Repugnance is the feeling that the audience should have for the villain. All the same such soliloquies are unique:

> Iago's soliloquies are designed to make him progressively more repellent. They are the hairpin bends by which we descend into the abyss of his nature.[10]

In brief, Iago tells us in his first soliloquy that he hates Othello and suspects that Othello has had an affair with his wife:

> I know not if't be true...
> Yet I, for mere suspicion in that kind,
> Will do, as if for surety.[11]

He also plans his "double knavery" in this soliloquy. In the second, he plans to gain the confidence of Othello and to poison his mind against Cassio. In the third, he plans to make Cassio and Roderigo drunk and set them against each other.

The audience is amazed as the plot of villainy gradually unfold in his mind, and sympathy is wholly alienated, as indeed, it should be.

The next five soliloquies are extremely important for the plot itself, not so much as indicative of character and mood.

Each of them takes the plot a step forward. The first of them is his fourth soliloquy (Act II, scene iii, ll. 327-53) in which he plans to make Desdemona plead for Cassio and to tell Othello that he is her lover. Thus we come to know the next step to be taken in the plot. In the fifth soliloquy, a short one (Act II, scene iii, ll. 372-78, p. 89), he plans to set Emilia pleading for Cassio to Desdemona while he takes Othello to a place where he can see Cassio requesting Desdemona to speak for him. In the 6th (Act III, scene iii, ll. 326-38, pp. 112-13), he decides to plant the handkerchief in Cassio's rooms. In the seventh (Act IV, scene i, ll. 93-103, pp. 140-41), he plans to question Cassio about Bianca in such a way that Othello will think that he is talking about Desdemona. This soliloquy is delivered after he has made Othello withdraw to a place from where he will be able to see and hear, while himself remaining invisible:

> As he shall smile, Othello shall go mad,
> And his unbookish jealousy must conster
> Poor Cassio's smiles, gestures and light behaviour,
> Quite in the wrong.[12]

In the last soliloquy, he plans to set Roderigo and Cassio against each other so that one may kill the other, or, with luck each kill the other (Act V, scene i, ll. 11-22, pp. 170-71). Each of these soliloquies is crucial to the plot and Coghill has, most appropriately, called them "signposts".

Shakespeare has, thus, gone against Elizabethan conventions in giving so many important soliloquies to the villain. But, then, whether, it is a matter of classical rules, or of contemporary conventions, he follows rules when it suits him and not otherwise. As Coleridge says:

> A pedant differed from a master in cramping himself with certain established rules, whereas the master regarded rules as always controllable by and subservient to the end.[13]

(c) The Sources of *Othello*

It was the custom for Elizabethan dramatists to take the material for their plays from many different works already in existence. Old plays, narrative poems, romances, histories and other documents were used to provide the story of the play. As far as Shakespeare is concerned the study of the sources from which he took his material for the plot has become an important branch of Shakespeare studies. It is highly instructive as well as illuminating to see how he selected the material from six or seven different sources, then rejected some, retained some, elaborated some and modified some in accordance with his needs. As Verity, in a slightly different context, has summed it up:

> His position is that of the Greek tragedians. He dealt with the existing material of drama...much as they dealt with the cycles of Greek traditional myth; and exercising the same sovereign liberty of appropriation, he turned it to the same inspired account.[14]

As far as *Othello* is concerned, however we do not have much choice of material, or much chance of admiring Shakespeare's ability to organise materials from different sources. The story comes from one source only, the seventh story in the third decade of Giraldi Cinthio's *Hecatommithi*. The original book in Italian was published in Venice in 1566. A French translation by Gabriel Chappuys was published in Paris in 1584. It is not known whether it was available not. It is not, either, known whether Shakespeare has enough knowledge of Italian or French to have read any of them. The first known English translation was published in 1753, so either there was an unlisted and unknown English translation which Shakespeare had consulted or somehow has had access to the Italian or the French version.

His ability to reorganise a story can be seen in his handling of Cinthio's romance. Here he was dealing with but one story but he brought his genius to bear on it so that the story might be made suitable for drama. There are at least eleven instances wherein he deviates from the original story.

First of all in Cinthio's story, the Moore (who remains nameless throughout) marries Desdemona and lives peacefully in Venice for some time. Shakespeare makes them start for Cyprus the very same night. The Ensign (Iago) falls in love with Desdemona and as she does not respond, thinks she has fallen in love with a Captain who is much valued by the Moore. Cinthio makes it clear that he really thinks Desdemona is in love with him:

> He imagined the reason [for Desdemona's lack of response to him] was that Desdemona had become enamoured of the Captain.[15]

In our play Iago is not in love with Desdemona, nor does he think her to be in love with Cassio. The loss of the handkerchief also is presented quite differently by Cinthio. According to him the Ensign:

> Had a little girl of three years old who was much loved by Desdemona, and one day while the poor lady was visiting this villain's house, he took the little girl in his arms and put her on the lady's lap...the trickster, who was surpassingly nimble-fingered, took the handkerchief from her girdle so cunningly that she did not notice.[16]

There are, in all, eleven such deviations from the original story in Shakespeare and in every instance the change makes the play dramatically more effective.

Most of the changes concern events, but there is another vital change. This concerns character. There is no such character as Roderigo in Cinthio. Shakespeare has invented this character, perhaps as a contrast to Iago and also to help explain Iago's personality and plottings which he reveals to Roderigo.

The most important changes concern the ending, whereby Shakespeare changes a sordid story into one of his finest tragedies. In Cinthio, the Moore does not commit suicide but is arrested on being charged by the Captain of having cut of his leg and murdered Desdemona. He is condemned to perpetual banishment and later killed by the kinsmen of Desdemona. Shakespeare transforms this ending, thereby giving us the great tragic figure of Othello.

(d) The Plot of *Othello*

The plot of *Othello* is much simpler than those of the other tragedies. Not only is it simpler, it is nearer to Aristotle's concept of tragedy than any of the others. After having given a brief account of the plots of *Hamlet*, *King Lear*, *Macbeth* and *Antony and Cleopatra*, M.R. Ridley comments:

> In none of them is that implication followed by explication...which Aristotle thought one of the features of great tragedy.... Shakespeare used this form only once in high tragedy and this is wherein *Othello* differs in structure and in effect from the others.[17]

He points out that if the first two Acts are treated as prologue then the play is seen as being better than all the other tragedies as far as classical requirements are concerned. This feature had been noticed by Dr. Johnson:

> Had the scene opened in Cyprus and the preceding incidents been occasionally related, there has been little wanting to a drama of the most exact and scrupulous regularity.[18]

Shakespeare's observance or lack of it, of the unities has already been commented upon in an earlier section of this chapter. Again, as far as multiplicity of plot goes, *Othello* is the most streamlined of all his tragedies. There is just one plot with many intrigues introduced by Iago. Indeed, without these intrigues the plot will not be able to proceed at all:

> The action and catastrophe of *Othello* depend largely on intrigues.[19]

This feature has been interpreted slightly differently by another critic who focusses on Iago:

> The structure of *Othello* develops in a series of improvised undeclared playlets in which Iago organises roles for his victims.[20]

In other words, *Othello* is a single-plotted play, thereby fulfilling one of the requirements of Aristotle: that tragedy is the imitation of one action, not of several. At the same time, this is different from the Elizabethan convention of double or multiple plots. There is no masterly interweavings of different plots as is to be seen in the other plays.

The plot of *Othello* has been, in spite of its simplicity, been interpreted in many different ways. Susan Snyder, one of the modern critics, gives paradoxical interpretation of its being partly a comedy:

> The whole story of comedy appears in *Othello* as preliminary to tragedy. The play's action up until the reunion of Othello and Desdemona in Cyprus is perfect comic structure in miniature.[21]

This is perfectly true—the first two Acts do represent, in a concentrated form, the movement of a comedy that comes to its peak in the ecstatic reunion at Cyprus. This critic takes the view that Shakespeare is questioning and evaluating the old assumptions of comedy, like love, marriage, etc., in *Othello* and the second half of the plot shows a tragic outcome.

Again, H.S. Wilson's grouping together of four plays as illustrating "the order of faith", *Romeo and Juliet*, *Hamlet*, *Othello* and *Macbeth* lays stress on the first two. He repeatedly brings *Romeo and Juliet* and *Othello* together, but he has not mentioned an important feature wherein the two radically differ from each other.

The difference lies in this: The plot of *Romeo and Juliet* shows a movement towards a direction opposite to that in *Othello*. Here we have a pair of lovers seeking union in spite of parental hostility. This union is not achieved and the play becomes a tragedy. *Othello*'s plot is very different. Here too we have parental opposition, but this is overcome and the lovers united right in the beginning. Then gradually the shadow of suspicion and jealousy darkens the play and the outcome is tragic. This dark shadow does not exist in *Romeo*. There the obstacles are all outer ones, and there is implicit faith between the lovers in the genuineness of love. In *Othello* once the knot has been tied, there are no outer obstacles. Even the Turkish threat vanishes away. Here the tragedy is brought about by inner obstacles,—obstacles that rise from the depths of the heart. Thus the play moves from blissful union to death. The play can be compared, in this respect, with *Antony and Cleopatra* as well. There also we have a united, blissfully happy couple in the beginning and then tragedy is brought about, as in *Romeo and Juliet*, by outward agencies.

Another view of the plot of Othello is that it is a complex but neat arrangement of contrasts and parallelisms. Each character is contrasted or balanced by another similar character. This brings about parallelism as well as contrast which go to make the pattern of the play. Thus Othello can be contrasted with Iago and is paralleled by Roderigo.

This is because both of them love Desdemona. Here there is contrast as well, for whereas Roderigo is a Venetian, Othello is a Moor. The most important contrast between the two is that whereas Othello kills Desdemona, Roderigo gives his life for her. Iago is contrasted with Othello, but also with Roderigo for he is a cold machiavellian whereas Roderigo is a fool. Like this there are contrasts and parallelisms to be found everywhere among the characters. All this makes for a complex structure.

This variety of opinions serves to point out the richness of Shakespeare's art. Even a play that is comparatively simple in theme and outline has brought forth a multiplicity of opinions on the most simple feature of it—the plot. After all the opinions are studied, it should be remembered that the plot is basically a simple one. As M.C. Bradbrook has declared:

> ...the well-knit appearance of a play like *Othello* is its own explanation.
>
> ... ...
>
> *Othello* is perhaps the most brilliantly constructed of all Elizabethan plays.[22]

References

1. Butcher, S.H., *op.cit.*, pp. 27-29.
2. *Ibid.*, p. 23.
3. Ridley, *op.cit.*, p. xlvii.
4. *Ibid.*, p. lxviii.
5. Act II, scene ii, l. 113, p. 74.
6. Act IV, scene i, ll. 84-86, p. 140.
7. Wain, *op.cit.*, p. 51.
8. *Ibid.*, p. 144.
9. *Ibid.*, p. 146. (Italics as in the original)
10. *Ibid.*
11. Act I, scene iii, ll. 386-88, p. 45.

12. Act IV, scene i, ll. 100-03, p. 141.
13. Wain, *op.cit.*, p. 54.
14. Verity, A.W., *Introduction to Hamlet*, Cambridge, 1989, Cambridge Univ. Press Indian edition, pp. xx-xxi.
15. Ridley, *op.cit.*, p. 239.
16. *Ibid.*, p. 242.
17. *Ibid.*, p. xlvi.
18. Wain, *op.cit.*, p. 51.
19. Bradley, *op.cit.*, p. 145.
20. Brennan, Anthony, in Wain, *op.cit.*, p. 188.
21. Bradbrook, *op.cit.*, pp. 14, 63.

10

Imagery and Symbolism

(a) Imagery

One of the embellishments that enhances the beauty of poetry is Imagery. Hand in hand with it goes symbolism. Modern critics have laid great stress on the different aspects of the poetic diction of Shakespeare, and imagery is one of them. The development of his imagery, its function, its relationship with the theme—all of these have been studied and analysed. H. Fluchère has given a definition of imagery which is a comprehensive one as well as succinct:

> Imagery may shortly be defined as a concrete illustration drawn upon by the poet to clarify or embellish the object that he seeks to describe.[1]

This is a very good definition, but Shakespeare's imagery cannot be contained within it. They are far richer and more complex. They go far beyond merely clarifying or embellishing an object. They carry out some other important functions as shall be discussed in this chapter.

Often enough it is difficult to differentiate between rhetorical figures, images and symbols. All three are integrally related and frequently overlap. An image is usually a figure of speech as well and may often be elevated to the status of a symbol. Fluchère explains it thus:

> No strict rule allows us to say at what point we pass from the plane of pure rhetoric to the plane of pure psychology and even the metaphysical plane, in the use of imagery.[2]

There are, moreover, different categories of images and the same image may belong to several different categories. A sense image may also be a domestic image, an astral image, or any other. This is a quality shared by all images.

Sense-images are the ones that are most obvious. Corresponding to the five human senses, there are five kinds of sense-images. Thus, corresponding respectively to the eye, the ear, the nose the tongue and the skin, there are visual, auditory, gustatory and tactile images.

Sometimes there might be a mixing and mingling of different sense-images, known as synaesthesia.

We shall look at the images in only one scene of the play, the third scene of the third Act, and try to analyse some of them. This is the longest scene and one of the two central ones. In fact it can be regarded as the central scene as the preceding one is the shortest. This will give the serious student an idea of the wealth of imagery in the entire play. It has been pointed out by H.S. Wilson that the imagery of *Othello* is not interpretive of the action so much as of character. The images used by a character explain his mood and mind, not the situation:

> The effect of imagery of *Othello* is dramatic, not choral. The imagery heightens the dramatic effect of the characters in action but it does not interpret the action for us.[3]

Here he is but repeating what Clemen had said two decades earlier in the very beginning of his chapter on *Othello*:

> We shall try to show Shakespeare's art of adapting imagery to the character using it, so that imagery becomes a means of characterising the *dramatis personae*.[4]

We shall, as has been said above, concentrate on one scene, but if a particularly important kind of image has to be illustrated, examples will be taken from elsewhere as well.

All the five kinds of sense-images can be found in this scene. One of the first remarkable sense-images is given by Cassio:

> Or feed upon such nice and wat'rish diet.[5]

Had the image been more detailed than in addition to being gustatory it would have taken on more qualities. For example, if Cassio had described a diet of milk and bread, describing the whiteness of the milk and the softness of the bread then the image would have been visual and tactile as well as gustatory.

A few lines later, Desdemona makes use of a visual image which is also an image dealing with falconry:

> I'll watch him tame and talk him out of patience.[6]

Here the visual quality is not very effective. A far more effective visual image occurs in Iago's famous description of jealousy:

> It is the green-ey'd monster, which doth mock
> That meat it feeds on.[7]

This image is a complex one, for it is a visual image, describing a monster. It is also a gustatory image, as it describes the monster feeding. It is an animal image, as it is about a non-human creature and finally it is a concrete description of the abstract idea of jealousy.

Both tactile and auditory images occur in Iago's false description of Cassio dreaming:

> In sleep I heard him say "sweet Desdemona,
> Let us be wary, let us hide our love."
> And then, sir, would he gripe and wring my hand.[8]

It may be objected that these are not images, for he says he actually heard Cassio talk and act as he did. Both are imaginary, and, moreover, they are being recounted to Othello as a series of images, so they can be treated as such.

Next to sense-images, nature images are the most prominent in Shakespeare. This kind of imagery includes all images related to nature. Shakespeare more than any other Elizabethan dramatist is known for his unparalleled wealth of nature imagery. Dryden had called attention to it:

> All the images of nature were still present to him and he drew them not laboriously but luckily; when he describes anything, you more than see it, you feel it too.[9]

This scene does not contain many nature images, but the few it does have are extraordinarily effective ones:

> Not poppy, nor mandragora
> Nor all the drowsy syrups of the world
> Shall ever medicine thee to that sweet sleep
> Which thou owedst yesterday.[10]

Both poppy and mandragora are images taken from the vegetable world and so are nature images, but this passage also contains a medical image ("drowsy syrups") which makes it so effective.

One of the most effective nature images has been used by Othello in his famous Homeric simile about the Pontic sea:

Like to the Pontic sea,
Whose icy current and compulsive course,
Ne'er feels retiring ebb, but keeps due on
To the Propontic and the Hellespont.[11]

This is a tremendous nature image, extremely dynamic. It is also a visual image, for the sea is meant to be seen. In addition it is also a tactile image, because of the "icy current".

Cosmic images are related to nature images. Generally this term is used to designate the images that involve planets, galaxies, etc. One such image is used in this scene by Othello:

And when I love thee not
Chaos is come again.[12]

Usually images are related to the senses. It is rare, almost impossible, to find an image that is unrelated to the senses. This is one such image, since chaos is something that cannot be apprehended by physical senses. It is beyond them. A remarkable cosmic image occurs in a late scene:

Methinks it should now be a huge eclipse
Of sun and moon, and that the affrighted globe
Should yawn at alteration.[13]

This is indeed an awe-inspiring cosmic image. No less than three heavenly bodies are concerned, and a cataclysm is described in three lines.

Images taken from different spheres of life are very common. One such kind, so prevalent in Shakespeare as to be almost imperceptible, consists of religious images. It is not that such images call attention to themselves, except in special cases. This is because the English language is permeated by references to the Bible and in poetry usually such references call up images. One such image occurs when Desdemona describes how she will importune Othello for Cassio's reinstatement:

His bed shall seem a school his board a shrift.[14]

Shrift is a confessional. Thus this becomes a religious image though it passes by almost unnoticed.

Another such instance of a religious image is to be found in the swear-word "Zounds". It has been used many times in this play. For example Othello uses it later in this scene (p. 102). It is an abbreviated form of the phrase "God's wounds", referring to the wounds received by Christ and as such is full of intense religious implications.

Images from the legal profession are not lacking. In this scene itself there is one. Iago makes use of it in the temptation scene:

who has a breast so pure,
But some uncleanly apprehensions
Keep lets and law-days, and in session sit
with meditations lawful?[15]

Here there are two images, one of a court of law, and the other of judges sitting in session.

Images from the world of sport abound. In this scene, there are two images from the sport of hawking. One used by Desdemona quoted above as illustration of visual imagery. Another, a much more detailed one, is used by Othello:

If I do prove her haggard,
Though that her jesses were my dear heart-stings,
I'ld whistle her off, and let her down the wind.[16]

Purely domestic images, as those related to household activities like cooking, washing, etc. and household articles are also used. When Desdemona first pleads for Cassio, she makes use of several of them with great effect:

Why, this is not a boon,
'Tis as I should entreat you wear your gloves:
Or feed on nourishing dishes, or keep you warm.[17]

The most famous domestic image of course, is that of the handkerchief. It is an example of an image developed into a symbol. When we see the actual handkerchief it is not an image, but after that, whenever it is referred to, it is not only an image;

it quickly develops in a symbol as has been explained in the section below. Let us, in the present instance, look upon it as an image. As such, it is a domestic image, concerned with dressing because usually it is looked upon as an accessory to one's dress. At first it is not even called a handkerchief but a napkin. About this M.R. Ridley has commented in the footnote to the line in which it occurs first:

> *Napkin* in general, any piece of "napery", but in Shakespeare always specifically a handkerchief.[18]

At this time it is a concrete object, not specifically described, so it can hardly be called an image. It becomes a colourful visual image when Iago describes it: "a handkerchief, spotted with strawberries".[19]

In the next few scenes the image grows and develops into a complex image-cum-symbol. In fact it becomes more of a symbol than an image and as such will be studied more in detail below.

There are many images having to do with different trades. There are many about medical treatment and one of them occurs in the famous "mandragora" passage quoted above, in which medical treatment for sleeplessness is talked about.

As Othello is a soldier, images having to do with the profession of soldiering abound in the play. The famous "farewell" speech is full of military images of all kinds.

> Farewell the neighing steed, and the shrill trumpet,
> The spirit-stirring drum, the ear piercing fife:
> The royal banner and all quality.[20]

As far as the senses are concerned, the images here combine visual and auditory qualities in addition to being military images.

Images having to do with classical myths are very common in Shakespeare. In plays having a classical background like *A Midsummer Night's Dream*, *Antony and Cleopatra*, *Troilus and Cressida,* etc. they are extraordinarily pervasive. In the present play also there are many, in this scene there are two, both used by Othello. One occurs towards the end of the farewell speech:

> And O ye mortal engines, whose wide throats
> The immortal Jove's great clamour counterfeit.[21]

He is describing the cannons used in the battlefields and compares them with the thunderbolt of Jove. So this is a classical image, visual and auditory and a military one in addition. The second classical image comes a few lines later:

> Her name, that was as fresh
> As Dian's visage, is now begrim'd and black.[22]

Diana, who is the moon-goddess as well as the goddess of chastity, is known for her silvery fair shining countenance. So here the image is a classical as well as a visual one.

Certain features of Shakespeare's imagery call for our attention. One of them is the accumulation of images. Shakespeare, in order to highlight any idea, uses more than one image. He uses several images in quick succession. For example, in the passage from the farewell speech given above, there are five images in three lines. The actual passage is much longer, consisting of ten lines and contains ten images. Here the images are all military ones. In another passage by Iago, there is an accumulation of animal images:

> Were they as prime as goats, as hot as monkeys,
> As salt as wolves, in pride; and fools as gross
> As ignorance made drunk.[23]

There are four images here in three lines and three of them are animal images. They are also visual images.

One of the remarkable features of Shakespeare's imagery is the repetition of the same kind of images throughout the play. Caroline Spurgeon calls them "iterative images". Such images help to create the atmosphere of a play and throw light on the mood of a character. In other words, in such cases imagery ceases to be merely decorative and becomes highly functional and integral to the play. Indeed, this is one of the many valuable points made by Wolfgang Clemen, that in his early plays the images are decorative, but as his art matured, his imagery also matured and become functional and more intimately related to the play itself:

> The images adapt themselves more and organically to the structural form of the drama.[24]

Clemen has pointed out several functions carried out by images as for example anticipation of future events, creation of atmosphere, characterisation, providing contrast, underlining of some thought and ideas, etc. As iterative images occur throughout the play, they carry out almost all of these functions. For example, images concerned with war is one of the iterative images used in this play. They occur from the very first scene to the last. In this scene also there are many of them. The first such is used, most unexpectedly, by Desdemona, pleading for Cassio:

> Save that, they say, the wars must make examples
> Out of their best.[25]

The most remarkable passage of war imagery is the farewell speech which contains, in all, ten war images in as many lines. These iterative images carry out the function of creating an atmosphere of conflict of giving an impression of the martial quality of the persons collected in Cyprus, of affording a glimpse into the speaker's character, etc. Other such groups of iterative images exist in imagery concerned with animals and diseases. The diligent student may study them at leisure.

Clemen has also described a complex feature of Shakespeare's images which he calls "imagery-consciousness". This is a kind of hidden image;

> The image which is merely suggested is a further sign of the intensive penetration of the language by the "imagery-consciousness".[26]

In other words the image is implied, not fully expressed. They, too, occur throughout the play and are so common that the reader is apt to pass them by, not realising that an image is implied. As Clemen says:

> The whole image has sunk beneath the surface, as it were, and has left behind it only one or two ideals concerned with it.[27]

For example, when Desdemona talks about pleading for Cassio she says:

> I'll watch him tame, and talk him out of patience.[28]

Here she is talking of the art of training a hawk or a falcon, but the image has not been clearly expressed. Such images are usually known as "hidden images" though Clemen uses a different term. They are very common, indeed, every time a brief metaphor comes, one can say there is an instance of "imagery-consciousness":

Caroline Spurgeon has given another term to describe the richness of Shakespeare's images: "image-complex". This refers to Shakespeare's preference for images concerned with certain activities or spheres of life; about gardening, sailing, astronomy, etc. In many cases these images are not clarified, but referred to in passing:

> Certain classes of thing, certain qualities in things, and certain aspects of life.[29]

There are many such in the play and in this scene. The first such is used by Cassio:

> Bounteous madam,
> Whatever shall become of Michael Cassio,
> He's never anything but your true servant.[30]

Here in the short phrase "true servant" the entire rich and complex tradition of the life-style of chivalry, of knight-errantry is suggested. Cassio's attitude to Desdemona is that of the devoted knight in the chivalric romances.

There are many other important features of Shakespeare's imagery. Examples in this discussion have been taken from one scene only. This would give the diligent student an idea of the richness and complexity of his imagery.

(b) Symbolism

As has been pointed out, just as, often a metaphor becomes an image, so, very often, an extra-ordinary image of an object, or the object itself, may develop into a symbol. Symbols or symbolic objects have a depth and a scope of meaning that cannot be paralleled by any other literary device. Symbols go out beyond the obvious meaning of the word or the object used, spreading out to give it a wider, deeper significance. They have been classified into different categories by different writers, and defined in many different ways. The definitions given by such poets who have themselves used symbols are of special significance, as, for example, those given by Coleridge and Yeats. The former, fore example, thinks that a symbol is organically linked with the thing for which it stands. It is no mere substitution. Several different characteristics of symbols have also been given.

Definitions or classifications of symbols were not available to Shakespeare, for it is a modern development. Such definitions or classifications would not be irrelevant when studying Shakespeare for such things are but tools which enable us to appreciate him better. No such classification or definition however, has been followed in the present work.

The most obvious symbol in *Othello*, of course, is Desdemona's handkerchief, but symbolic qualities have been found in the characters as well. G. Wilson Knight is the most prominent among those critics who impose symbolic value on the main characters. He calls this "triple symbolism". Analysing the character of Othello he says:

> Therefore Othello, with reference to the Shakespearian universe, becomes automatically, a symbol of faith in the human values of love, of war, of romance in a wide and sweeping sense.[31]

It is noticeable that he gives a highly positive interpretation of this symbolism he finds in Othello. To most readers, Othello may stand for a symbol of jealousy. Wilson Knight does not consider this aspect of Othello. He neglects this unpleasant side of his character altogether.

Taking the character of Desdemona, he finds her a symbol of women in general:

> Now Desdemona, also very human, with an individual dominant feminine charm and simplicity, is yet also a symbol of women in general, daring the unknown sea of marriage with the mystery of man.[32]

Here again, all the readers may not agree. If Desdemona is to be treated as a symbol, she can stand for chastity and pure, unselfish love, for with her last breath (literally) she tries to save Othello.

Wilson Knight finds symbolic value in Iago as well. To him, Iago is mainly a man of intellect. He sets himself against Othello (symbolising love and romance), and Desdemona (symbolising married women), for no satisfactory reason. Knight finds in him:

> Cynicism loathing beauty, refusal to allow its existence...Iago is cynicism incarnate and projected into action.[33]

H.S. Wilson agrees with this view of Iago and treats him as a symbol.

> Iago admirably symbolises the negativeness of everything.[34]

This investing of the main characters with symbolic values is not accepted by all. Nearly thirty years later a notably thoughtful critic disagrees with it. Robert Ornstein refuses to ascribe symbolic qualities to characters. He says that each character is highly individualistic, with particular instincts about his personality, his past, and his present and we must not ignore this fact:

> When we ignore this particularity and attempt to make universal or symbolic figures of the characters in Othello we only distort them.[35]

There has been no hesitation, however, in ascribing symbolic value to inanimate objects and objects of nature, whether animate or not. Two such symbols that Wilson Knight finds prevalent in Shakespeare are: storms symbolising violence and disintegration and music, signifying harmony. In this play, a storm has been described in the beginning of Act II. It is just described, not presented on the stage as in *King Lear* or in *The Tempest*. Knight says:

> Storms are continually symbols of tragedy in Shakespeare.[36]

In the description given by Cassio, the storm is seen to be sensible of and responsive to Desdemona's beauty:

> Tempests themselves, high seas and rocking winds,
> The gutter'd rocks and congregated sands,
> Traitors ensteeped to clog the guiltless keel,
> As having sense of beauty, do omit
> Their mortal natures, letting go safely by
> The divine Desdemona.[37]

This is a highly positive view of the storm, but its strength is not to be dismissed lightly. A few lines earlier the Second Gentleman accompanying Montano describes the force of the storm:

> The chiding billow seems to pelt the clouds,
> The wind-shak'd surge, with high and monstrous main,
> Seems to cast water on the burning bear
> And quench the guards of the ever-fixed pole.[38]

This storm in the world of nature blows over, but it is prophetic of the psychological storm that is to take place:

> The storm of sea or bruit of cannonade are powerless to hurt them; yet there is another storm brewing in the venomed mind of Iago.[39]

The later critics also agree with this view. Nevill Coghill points out that the invention of the storm was not at all necessary. Why, then, did Shakespeare invent it at all? He asks:

> was it to symbolise the inward storm about to break over and separate them till death?[40]

This particular scene does not contain the symbol of a storm in the world of nature, but definitely the psychological storm has already been called up by Iago. Othello is storm-tossed by doubt and jealousy and at the end of the scene, he is taking the vow of revenge.

Next we come to the most important symbol in this play: the Handkerchief. Many critics have objected to Shakespeare's giving so much importance to such an insignificant object. Rymer is one of them:

> So much ado, so much stress, so much passion and repetition about an Handkerchief! Why was not this call'd the *Tragedy of the Handkerchief*? ...the Handkerchief is so remote a trifle, no Booby on this side Mauretania cou'd make consequence from it.[41]

The French dramatist Jean-Francois Ducis found it so offensive that in his version of the play he changed it into a diamond bracelet.

The handkerchief is brought in casually enough in this very scene. Othello pretends to have a headache and Desdemona offers to bind up his forehead with her handkerchief. It is not even called a handkerchief at first (vide Ridley's comment quoted above). When Desdemona drops it, the term "handkerchief" is used in the stage-direction. Then, talking to Iago, Emilia uses it and thereafter this is the term used and gradually takes on symbolic value.

It starts taking on symbolic dimensions when Iago mentions to Othello that he has seen it in Cassio's hands. This is the "ocular proof" that Othello wanted, and this marks the turning-point in Othello's mind. He becomes convinced of Desdemona's infidelity. This is not as surprising as it appears. A handkerchief was regarded as a status symbol in those days, as aristocrats used them. Moreover:

> In *cinquecento* Venice, possession of a lady's handkerchief was considered proof of adultery and led to stringent punishment.[42]

This critic cites a legal case in which a man named Tomaso Querini was sentenced to eighteen months imprisonment and a fine of 500 lire. Records of the case tell how this man first got the handkerchief of a lady and thereafter committed adultery with her. It is not surprising that Othello should take it as "proofs of holy writ".

Then, as time goes on, its symbolic value comes clearer and clearer. It takes on magical properties when Othello describes it in the next scene. He tells her that it has the property of making the husband of the woman who possesses it adore her, but this adoration will turn to hated if she lost it:

> There's magic in the web of it;
> A sybil, that had number'd in the world
> The sun to make two hundred compasses,
> In her prophetic fury sew'd the work.[43]

He gives her more details about the silk, the worms that wove the silk, etc. In other words, he puts the fear of God into her. This becomes all the more pronounced when he wants to see it:

> Oth.: Is't lost? is't gone? Speak, is it out o' the way?
> Des.: Heaven bless us!
> Oth.: Say you?... ... ...
> ... ...
> Oth.: The handkerchief !
> Des.: I pray, talk me of Cassio.
> Oth.: The handkerchief![44]

In fact, from line 45 to 98 the word "handkerchief" is used seven times. These lines are all devoted to it. By this time it has assumed symbolic proportions. As Wilson Knight points out:

> Note too the significance of the magic handkerchief *as both a symbol of domestic sanctity and the play's one link with the supernatural.*[45]

Karen Newman finds a three-fold symbolism in it: historical, psychological and political:

> The handkerchief therefore is not significant only historically as an indicator of class or transgression or psychologically because it signifies male fears of duplicity...but also politically precisely because it has become a *feminine* trifle.[46]

There is thus a gender-based symbolism implied in it also, though handkerchiefs were used by men as well as women. Feminine handkerchiefs however could be easily distinguished from masculine ones.

At the play goes on the symbolic value of the item intensifies rather than diminishes. When at the point of killing Desdemona, Othello again talks about it:

> That handkerchief which I so lov'd and gave thee
> Thou gavest to Cassio.

... ...

By heaven, I saw my handkerchief in his hand.[47]

It is mentioned again and again in the rest of the scene by Othello and Emilia who finally resolves the mystery by disclosing how she found it and gave it to Iago. The handkerchief thus brings about the death not only of Desdemona but of Othello and Emilia as well. Carol Thomas Neely, like Karen Newman, says:

> The lost handkerchief becomes the emblem of the women's power and its loss.[48]

As this discussion shows, Othello is extremely rich in imagery of various kinds, but not so rich in symbolism. Even then, the one major symbol it contains has passed into the realm of undoubted and complex symbols that yield a wealth of different interpretations. It cannot be doubted however, that Shakespeare's strength lay in images, not in symbols. Perhaps this was because he did not make conscious use of symbols as, for example, Yeats did—it is later critics who have found symbolic value in certain objects or characters in his plays.

References

1. Fluchère, *op.cit.*, p. 167.
2. *Ibid.*
3. Wilson, *op.cit.*, p. 67.
4. Clemen, Wolfgang, *The Development of Shakespeare's Imagery*, Methuen, London, 1977.
5. Act III, scene iii, l. 15, p. 94.
6. Act III, scene iii, l. 161, p. 162.
7. Act III, scene iii, ll. 170-71, p. 103.
8. Act III, scene iii, ll. 425-27, p. 119.
9. Enright, D.J. and Chickera, Ernst de, ed., *English Critical Texts*, Oxford Univ. Press, 2002, p. 88.
10. Act III, scene iii, ll. 335-37, p. 113.
11. Act III, scene iii, ll. 460-63, p. 121.
12. Act III, scene iii, ll. 92-93, p. 98.
13. Act V, scene ii, ll. 100-02, p. 183.
14. Act III, scene iii, l. 24, p. 95.
15. Act III, scene iii, ll. 142-45, p. 101.

16. Act III, scene iii, ll. 264-66, p. 109.
17. Act III, scene iii, ll. 77-79, p. 97.
18. Ridley, *op.cit.*, p. 111 fn.
19. Act III, scene iii, ll. 41-42, p. 102.
20. Act III, scene iii, ll. 357-59, p. 114.
21. Act III, scene iii, ll. 361-62, p. 114.
22. Act III, scene iii, ll. 392-93, p. 117.
23. Act III, scene iii, ll. 409-11, p. 118.
24. Clemen, Wolfgang, *The Development of Shakespeare's Imagery*, London, Methuen, and Co. Ltd., 1977, p. 74.
25. Act III, scene iii, ll. 60-67, p. 96.
26. Clemen, *op.cit.*, p. 77.
27. *Ibid.*
28. Act III, scene iii, l. 23, p. 94.
29. Spurgeon, Caroline, *Shakespeare's Imagery and What it Tells us.* Cambridge, Univ. Press, 1935, p. 44.
30. Act III, scene iii, ll. 7-9, p. 94.
31. Knight, G. Wilson, *op.cit.*, p. 107.
32. *Ibid.*, p. 109.
33. *Ibid.*, p. 114.
34. Wilson, *op.cit.*, p. 61.
35. Ornstein, Robert, *The Moral Vision of Jacobean Tragedy*, Madison, The University of Toronto Press, 1960, p. 228.
36. Knight, *op.cit.*, p. 109.
37. Act II, scene i, ll. 67-63, pp. 51-52.
38. Act II, scene i, ll. 11-15, pp. 47-48.
39. Knight, *op.cit.*, p. 111.
40. Wain, *op.cit.*, p. 150.
41. *Ibid*, p. 45.
42. Newman, Karen, *Femininity and the Monstrous in Othello*, in Wain, *op.cit.*, p. 216. (*Cinquecento* means an adjective of "the fifteenth century.")
43. Act III, scene iv, ll. 64-67-70, p. 127.
44. Act III, scene iv, ll. 78-91, p. 128.
45. Knight, *op.cit.*, p. 109. Italics as in the original.
46. Newman, *op.cit.*, p. 218.
47. Act V, scene ii, ll. 48-63, p. 180.
48. Wain, *op.cit.*, p. 98.

11

Poetic Style: Diction and Versification

It is always been taken for granted that poetry has two aspects: the thoughts and emotions expressed, and the style. The poetic style of our dramatist has been studied in great detail. Not only does his style reflect his age (i.e., it is an Elizabethan-Jacobean style), it reflects his own personality as well. Again, the style is suited to each of the characters. Such achievements are truly miraculous.

Shakespeare's plays, as was the prevailing custom, were written in a mixture of prose and verse. The noble characters, (usually those in the main plot), speak in poetry and the humbler ones in prose. There are many exceptions to this rule as well, according to the situation in the play. Moreover, it should be borne in mind that poetic style does not mean only the language used, the phrase often covers versification as well. These two aspects shall be now studied in turn.

(a) Poetic Diction

There is a rich classical tradition about this aspect of poetry and the Elizabethans were quite familiar with it, specially the theories of the Roman writers. Horace had put down the rules of poetic diction quite clearly in his *Ars Poetica*. The diction of different kinds of poetry should vary and so should that of the characters speaking. For example, the diction of elegies should be different from that of love lyrics. In drama, the characters should speak in conformity with their (a) age, (b) sex, and (c) social status:

> It will make a great difference whether a god or a hero is speaking, a man of ripe years or a hot-headed youngster

> in the pride of youth, a woman of standing or an officious nurse, a roving merchant or a prosperous farmer.[1]

In this one famous sentence, Horace has provided for all differences in the speeches of the *dramatis personae* of all kinds. Distinction is made between the divine and the mortal. Then among humans, there are hundreds of varieties and diction must be adjusted to all these. Age must be taken into account ("man of ripe years or a hot-headed youngster") and so must sex ("woman of standing"). Within these basic categories there are many other divisions according to age and social position. Horace differentiates between "a woman of standing or an officious nurse". A classic example of both are Lady Capulet and Nurse in *Romeo and Juliet*. He also differentiates among the different professions: "roving merchant" and a "prosperous farmer". These categories, naturally, can be added to *ad infinitum*. In other words, the language must suit the speaker. Accordingly, in later Elizabethan drama, diction became highly specialised. As M.C. Bradbrook has declared:

> The specific style for princes, for lovers, for clowns, was fixed.[2]

The poet should, however, keep in mind certain general maxims—whichever variety of style he might be using. Not only must the diction be realistic in accordance with the speaker's personality, it must also be such as to persuade the reader or the audience and at the same time move him emotionally:

> The Elizabethan dramatist's style is one of impassioned poetic rhetoric, the two commonest functions of which are to persuade and to touch the emotions.[3]

It has also been pointed out by classical rhetoricians and theorists that a poet should make use of rhetorical figures. Aristotle, in his definition of tragedy, points out that the language is properly embellished in different places. The style may be the grand, or the middle, or even the low style, but it should make use of rhetorical figures. Ben Jonson's incomparable play *The Alchemist* is an ideal example of the low style. Here most of the characters come from a low strata in society and the diction is the low style. When the only aristocrat Sir Epicure Mammon speaks, Jonson switches over to the grand style. But, whether it is the knight speaking or Face the servant, Jonson uses figures of speech.

There was no dearth of English theorists either. They too followed the classical critics. George Puttenham is the best-known of them. He says:

> There is nothing so fitte for the poem as to be furnished with all the figures that be Rhetoricall and such as do most beautifie the language with eloquence.[4]

Many theories of diction have been expounded by classical and later rhetoricians. In his famous theory of poetic diction, for example, Horace tells the young poet to use newly-coined words as well as out-of-mode words. Shakespeare was fully acquainted with these ideas and used them, according to his own convenience. Here again, he was no stickler for rules, and, as with the different aspects of his drama, his style too developed as he himself grew. The style of Othello is a mature one.

(i) Diction in Othello

Shakespeare's dramatic career stretched over quite a long period, over two decades in fact. This is a period of continuous development for him. His art conquered new territories as the years passed and riper years reached higher peaks of excellence. Not only did his art of characterisation and plot-management develop, but so did his style and versification.

Moreover, he takes within his stride all the conventions of style as prevalent in Elizabethan drama and shows how they can be used to serve his own artistic purposes. The use of a mixture of prose and verse serves to distinguish the noble from the humble characters. It was also one of the requirements of poetic diction that the language should be in harmony with the action taking place on the stage. As Aristotle declares, tragedy should use:

> ...language enriched in a variety of ways and artistic devices appropriate to the several parts of the play.[5]

In other words, even the same character must not speak in the same manner in different situations. In the play under discussion, Iago illustrates this point the most obviously. He speaks to Roderigo in a manner very different from the way he speaks to Othello or to Desdemona. In his soliloquies, again, he speaks in a totally different manner. Othello, when speaking in the drunken scene when dismissing Cassio, speaks very differently from the manner in which he defends himself to the senators, or in his farewell speech. Shakespeare had mastered the art of modulating his diction by the time that he wrote this play and the diction is always in keeping with the occasion. Some of the stylistic devices used in the play shall now be studied.

(ii) Stylistic Devices

Stylistic devices are of many kinds, ranging from the extremely obvious to the infinitely complex. Of these, imagery, symbols and figures of speech are the most important. The first two have already been discussed, though in a sketchy manner, in the preceding chapter. Some of the important figures of speech and other devices will be now taken up. As it is not possible to study the whole play from this point of view, only one scene, the third scene of the third Act, will be studied, as was done in the foregoing chapter. It should always be remembered that the diction in *Othello* is very rich in the entire play. Isolating just one scene will never be enough of a satisfactory study. It can only serve as pointer. The diction of the play is so rich that Wilson Knight has called it "the Othello music".

> The noble *Othello* music; highly-coloured, rich in sound phrase, stately.[6]

It is specially Othello's own speeches that have called forth this encomium. Othello's speeches indeed merit special attention. His use of proper nouns and of military images should be studied in detail by the diligent student.

Metaphors and similes attract the attention of the reader very easily, and of them similes are the most obvious. One of the most well-known similes in this scene is used by Iago:

> trifles light as air
> Are to the jealous, confirmations strong
> As proofs of holy writ.[7]

This simile has become all the more effective because in it two mutually contrasted things have been taken for comparison.

The "trifles" are light, but "holy writ" is something extremely serious. Yet the simile perfectly corresponds to the real life situation it illustrates. Desdemona's handkerchief is a light but it is going to produce a jealousy that will lead to her murder.

There is an example of accumulated similes in one of Iago's speeches to Othello about "ocular proof":

> Were they as prime as goats, as hot as monkeys,
> As salt as wolves, in pride; and fools as gross
> As ignorance made drunk.[8]

Here we have four similar piled up onto each other in three lines. This accumulation of similes (which is also an accumulation of images) is a very common feature of Shakespeare's poetry.

Homeric similes are well-known for the grandeur with which they invest poetry. The best known Homeric simile in the play is in this scene:

> Like to the Pontic sea,
> Whose icy currents and compulsive course,
> Ne'er feels retiring ebb, but keeps due on
> To the Propontis and the Hellespont:
> Even so my bloody thoughts and violent pace
> Shall ne'er look back; ne'er ebb to humble love,
> Till that a capable and wide revenge
> Swallow them up.[9]

This is a simile elaborated over eight lines and is extremely apt since a current of the sea has been compared with bloody thoughts which themselves flow in currents. The simile is far more complex and needs further study to reveal its beauties.

Metaphors have always been regarded very seriously by rhetoricians. Indeed, Longinus devotes an entire chapter to it. They are of many different kinds but all of them are not to be found in this scene. One of the most important metaphors in the entire play is used by Iago:

> O beware jealousy:
> It is the green-ey'd monster, which doth mock
> That meat it feeds on.[10]

Though short, it is an extremely important passage. The complexity of the image used has already been pointed out (vide

Chapter 10 *supra*). In addition to all this, it uses another figure of speech, synecdoche, which will be explained later. Its prosodic peculiarities will be pointed out in the relevant section.

Similes and metaphors are figures based on resemblance, but figures based on difference are not lacking in the scene either. One such figure is that of antithesis and we come across one of them quite early when Desdemona is describing Cassio:

> For if he be no one that truly loves you,
> That errs in ignorance and not in cunning
> I have no judgment in an honest face.[11]

Antitheses are usually concentrated in one line. Here that is the case with the second line (line no. 50 in the text), but it takes in the line before and after it as well. Later on we have a clearer case of anti-thesis:

> I think my wife be honest, and think she is not
> I think that thou art just, and think thou art not.[12]

Here the two antitheses in the two consecutive lines are far more pointed than in the former example, emphasising the conflict in Othello.

The first important figure of speech used in this scene is that of apostrophe, when Cassio first addresses Desdemona:

> Bounteous madam,
> Whatever shall become of Michael Cassio,
> He's never anything but your true servant.[13]

Besides containing an apostrophe, this passage also has special features in imagery, as has been pointed out in the relevant chapter. This scene contains many remarkable apostrophes. Two of the most important are to be found in the oath-taking scene. Othello apostrophises Revenge and Love and his own chest:

> Arise, black vengeance, from thy hollow cell,
> Yield up, O love, thy crown and hearted throne,
> To tyrannous hate, swell, bosom, with thy fraught,
> For 'tis of aspic's tongues![14]

Here there are three apostrophes in three-and-half lines. Such wealth of quick succession of apostrophes are very rare.

These are usually looked upon as apostrophes, but a strict rhetorician would call them invocations. The farewell speech is also an example of apostrophe but not such a clear example as the one given above. Iago's oath-taking passage which follows a few lines later is also a splendid example of apostrophe.

Hyperboles also, like apostrophes contribute to the magnificence of a passage. Many of them are scattered throughout the play. One of the most well-known of them occurs just before the temptation scene. Othello says about Desdemona:

> Excellent wretch! Perdition catch my soul
> But I do love thee, and when I love thee not
> Chaos is come again.[15]

This passage, though a very short one, is extremely effective. Not only does it contain a hyperbole, but a few other figures of speech that have not been mentioned so far. First of all, we think there is a hyperbole in the concept of chaos coming if he ceases to love Desdemona, but later it is seen to be the actual fact he is stating, for when he falls down in a fainting fit, uttering disjoined words, chaos has truly come into his world. Thus, anticipating later events, this is a prolepsis.

Yet this does not fully account for the excellence of the passage. Its opening words contain a figure of speech that is the very opposite of hyperbole. It is a litote or understatement. The term "wretch", though a word with a negative meaning is used in a positive sense here. Thus we find two mutually opposite figures of speech in the same passage—exaggeration and understatement.

In addition, there is another figure of speech involved in the opening phrase "Excellent wretch". The two words are mutually contradictory. Thus it is an oxymoron.

As he is addressing Desdemona, the entire passage is regarded as an apostrophe. So the passage, within its two and a half lines, uses no less than five figures of speech: hyperbole, prolepsis, litote, oxymoron and apostrophe, adding piquancy to it. It is not surprising that this is one of the most effective passages in the play.

One of the figures of speech that, like apostrophe, enhances the dramatic quality of passage is the rhetorical question. Shakespeare makes lavish use of it in this scene. In the beginning of the scene, Desdemona uses four of them:

> I wonder in my soul,
> What you could ask me, that I should deny?
> Or stand so mammering on? What? Michael Cassio
> That came a-wooing with you.[16]

She ends the sentence beginning with "Michael Cassio" with another rhetorical question (the full sentence has not been quoted here). This makes her request to Othello very effective. But this use of rhetorical question is as nothing to the use our poet puts it to only a few lines later:

> Iago: Indeed?
> Oth.: Indeed? Indeed: discerns't thou ought in that?
> Is he not honest?
> Iago: Honest, my lord?
> Oth.: Honest? Ay, honest.
> Iago: My lord, for aught I know.
> Oth.: What dost thou think?
> Iago: Think, my lord?
> Oth.: Think, my lord?[17]

There are no less than nine questions in these nine lines, and the lines are mostly very short ones, not iambic pentameters. Besides, there is a mixture of straight questions and rhetorical questions, which goes to make the passage all the more effective.

Besides these few, there are numerous other figures of speech in the play, but rhetorical figures are not the only device used by a writer. There are allusions also, i.e. references to other works. These are of many different kinds. An author may refer to the Bible, to classical myths, to classical writers or their works, to contemporary events, etc. All of these are plentiful in Shakespeare. Biblical references are so much a part of his diction that they occur throughout the play, sometimes in a clear and distinct manner and sometimes in a less obtrusive but effective manner. One of the first kinds occurs when Iago tells Othello:

> My lord, you know I love you.[18]

This refers directly to a well-known sentence in St. John's Gospel. Jesus asks Peter whether he loved Him or not and Peter replies in all sincerity:

> Yea, lord, thou knowest that I love thee.[19]

This is repeated twice more, in verses 16 and 17, and therefore becomes extremely effective. Iago's sentence will at once remind the audience of St. Peter. A less clear but no less effective allusion occurs when Iago talks about the handkerchief:

> Trifles light as air
> Are to the jealous, confirmations strong
> As proofs of holy writ.[20]

Holy writ of course, refers to the scriptures.

Classical allusions can be of many types. There are references to classical myths, to classical authors and to literary works. Two mythical references occur in this scene, both given by Othello. One is in the farewell speech, referring to the sound of cannons:

> whose wide throats
> The immortal Jove's great clamour counterfeit.[21]

The other occurs when he talks of his reputation:

> My name, that was as fresh
> As Dian's visage, is now begrim'd and black.[22]

Both of these allusions make use of proper names and the use of proper names is a device that adds grandeur to poetry. The most remarkable use of proper names in this scene is to be found in Othello's famous speech.

> Like to the Pontic sea,
> Whose icy currents and compulsive course,
> Ne'er feels retiring ebb, but keeps due on
> To the Propontis and the Hellespont.[23]

Marlowe is well-known for his powerful use of proper names and these lines have often been called Marlovian in their effectiveness. These proper names with their majestic roll of sound and their associations, give the passage a grandeur that it might not have had otherwise. The passage, of course, contains several more lines. It has homeric simile with the prevalent image of the current in the sea being compared with the current of blood in arteries and views of humans.

Only a few of the rhetorical devices in but one scene has been mentioned here. The serious student of Shakespeare may spend an entire lifetime studying them in his different works.

(b) Versification

Poetic style has two aspects and one of them, the diction, has been studied, though in a very limited manner. A very cursory account of Shakespeare's versification shall now be given. A knowledge of prosody is essential for understanding this aspect of poetry. Henri Fluchère points out:

> It is by its rhythm as much as its images that a verse is expressive. The rhythmical succession has an emotional pattern, shows a purpose, imposing a mood or defining a thought.[24]

The usual medium of Elizabethan drama is blank verse, i.e., passages of unrhyming iambic pentameter lines. This is a very flexible meter and underwent many changes from early Elizabethan till late Jacobean drama. Given below is an example of regular blank verse:

T̆he pó/lĭcý/măy éi/thĕr lást/sŏ lońg/,
Ŏr feéd/ŭpón/sŭch níce/aňd ẃa/trĭsh diét/.
Ŏr bréed/ĭtsélf/sŏ oút/ŏf cír/cŭmstańce/,
Thăt Í/beĭng aб́/seňt ańd/my̆ pláce/sŭpplíed/.[25]

This passage has four lines, with no rhymes of any kind. All the lines are iambic pentameters. Such absolutely regular blank verse passages are difficult to find. There are usually other meters like trochees and anapaests, mixed with iambs to give flexibility to a passage of blank verse.

Versification has many complex features. Two of them are the use of end-stopped and of run-on lines. The former is the kind of line that requires the reader or the actor to make a definite pause at the end. Early Elizabethan used quite an amount of end-stopped blank verse which made such passages mechanical and monotonous as well as rather jerky. Thus in one of the well-known pre-Shakespearean play *Ralph Roister Doister*, is written mostly in end-stopped lines. The first four lines of the play run like this:

> As long liveth the merry man, they say,
> As doth the sorry man, and longer by a day;
> Yet the grasshopper, for all his summer piping,
> Starveth in winter with hungry griping.[26]

Every line in this passage has a punctuation mark denoting a pause at the end. In such cases the verse gives an impression of being stilted and also clumsy. At times however, end-stopped lines can be used deliberately for a specific purpose, as, for example, to emphasise certain lines or ideas. Our poet has used them, repeatedly, with great effect:

> Think, my lord? By heaven, he echoes me,
> As if there were some monster in his thought,
> Too hideous to be shown; thou didst mean something;
> I heard thee say but now, thou lik'st not that;
> When Cassio left my wife: what didst not like?[27]

Here Shakespeare has made the lines end-stopped ones in order to emphasise each of them. He stops briefly at the end of each line, as if puzzling out Iago's reactions to his questions.

The opposite of this is the run-on line, which is also known as enjambement. Here there is no stopping at the end of the line. Instead one line carries on smoothly into the next. Most good blank verse is of this kind. Desdemona, speaking to Cassio about his reinstatement, is assuring him that she will do her best for him:

> before Emilia here
> I give thee warrant of thy place I assure thee
> If I do vow a friendship, I'll perform it
> To the last article; my lord shall never rest,[28]

Here the actress does not have to pause at the end. Instead she moves on to the next line. If she has to pause to take breath, she can do so somewhere within the line. This not only gives the passage flexibility, but encourages the natural rhythm of conversation.

This feature of making a pause somewhere within the line is known as the caesura or the medial pause. Mediaeval verse, as it existed before the development of Elizabethan dramatic or declamatory blank verse, had a special feature: it had a pause in the middle of the line. This made for a very artificial and jerky rhythm. Shakespeare and the other Elizabethan writers varied the placing of the caesura from line to line, thus giving the passage flexibility. In the passage quoted above, provision has been made for the placing of the caesura by putting appropriate punctuation marks:

> Do not doubt that: || before Emilia here
> I give thee warrant of thy place; || assure thee
> If I do vow a friendship, || I'll perform it
> To the last article, || my lord shall never rest.[29]

Here the double vertical lines indicate the caesura. In the first line the caesura falls after the fourth syllable, but in the next line after the eighth. In the third line it falls after the seventh syllable and in the fourth after the fourth. Thus the actress shall stop for breath at different places in different lines. The lines accommodate themselves to the rise and fall of the speaker's voice.

Sometimes the writer may make use of more than one caesura in the same line for greater effect. Desdemona, on seeing Othello, asks Cassio to stay on and hear her speak for him. He however, haltingly excuses himself:

> Madam, || not now, || I am very ill at ease[30]

His hesitation is accentuated by two caesurae in the same line. A few lines late we have a line with three of them. Desdemona is speaking:

> Why || your lieutenant, || Cassio, || good my lord[31]

Here, instead of hesitation as in Cassio's line, the caesurae are used for emphasising the words after which they come. The caesura thus, is a very versatile device. Only three uses of it have been illustrated here, but there are more.

Blank verse lines, by definition, contain ten syllables, but this is a very flexible rule. Often enough, in order to vary the monotony of the lines, or to produce some special effects, the writer may use more, or less, than ten syllables.

> O, beware jealousy.[32]

This line, though it contains only six syllables, is counted as one full line. In contrast the following line has twelve syllables:

> Look where he comes, not poppy, nor mandragora.[33]

The most remarkable use of short lines occurs in Act III, scene iv where Othello is questioning Desdemona about the handkerchief. There are many lines in this dialogue which are much shorter than a pentameter, and the shortest is a monosyllabic line by Othello, consisting of just one word; "Ha"! Yet it has been counted as a full line. Such devices are used for special effects.

Another way of introducing variety in blank verse is the use of stichomythia. There are many varieties of this, one of which is breaking up a single line between different speakers:

> Iago: And when she seem'd to shake and fear your looks. She lov'd them most.
> Oth.: And so she did.
> Iago: Why, go to then.

Here the second line is a hexameter and has been broken up twice, to be delivered in three parts, by two speakers, it is however, counted as a single line. This device makes for great dramatic effect on stage.

Couplets too are used in Elizabethan play. There are two notable instances of entire passages in couplets in this play, none of them in this scene. The first occurs in Act I, scene iii. There are two passages of Senecan couplets, declaimed first by the Duke and next by Brabantio. There is a total of nine couplets between them, all of them in the manner of moral *sententiae* of Seneca. The Duke begins:

> When remedies are past, the grief are ended,
> By seeing the worst, what late on hopes depended.[34]

Brabantio ends the twin passages with an eminently practical view. The bereaved father closes up his heart's grief:

> But words are words; I never yet did hear
> That the bruis'd heart was pierced through the ear.[35]

These are typical Senecan couplets. The next notable passage of couplets occurs in Act II, scene i, in which Iago tosses off a series of doggerel rhymes for the entertainment of Desdemona.

Besides these, almost every scene ends with a couplet which either gives the theme or the state of the speaker's mind. The scene we have been dealing with so far (Act III, scene iii) is an exception from this point of view.

Songs are an important feature in the plays of Shakespeare. This play contains three of them. Music is one of the Aristotelian requirements of tragedies through the ages and Shakespeare's plays fulfill that need. Of the three, two are drinking songs sung by Iago, in Act II, scene iii, and the third is the famous willow-song sung by Desdemona.

Drinking songs are a well-known type of song, right from the classical times. It is one of the five kinds of lyrics mentioned by Horace. The god Bacchus is praised in classical songs which is not done in these. As the setting of the play is Italian, this could have been done. Instead the English king, King Stephen is described. The first song "and let me the cannikin clink" is a proper drinking song but the one about King Stephen is just a convivial song fit for the occasion.

Both of these are functional songs. It is not that Iago is merry himself. He only pretends to be so in order to produce the right atmosphere of jollification which will make Cassio drunk. The songs are sung with this end in view.

The willow-song is very different. It is so significant that the scene (Act IV, scene iii) is often named after it. Desdemona has had a most trying day. Othello has insulted her and struck her in a public place. He has treated her like a prostitute. Then, instead of resting, she had to attend a formal party. Now at last she is getting ready for bed. The sad willow-song has been haunting her. Her mother's maid used to sing it, and died, forsaken by her mad lover, with this song on her lips. So the song has extremely tragic implications. It is sorrowful from the very beginning and ends with the concept of marital infidelity. It begins by evoking pity:

> The poor soul sat sighing, by a sycamore tree,
> sing all a green willow:
> Her hand on her bosom, her head on her knee,
> sing willow, willow, willow.[36]

The song is in one stanza with the line "Sing willow, willow, willow" occurring after almost every line. Everything about the song is sad. It used to be sung by an unfortunate girl while dying; the refrain repeats the word "willow" which is associated sadness, being called weeping willow, associated with widows and graveyards. Moreover, the song has thirteen lines. Thus, in every way, it anticipates disaster, and creates the right mood for the scene of the murder. This scene and the song was invented by Shakespeare.

The different aspects of poetic style, as have been sketchily dealt with in this chapter, form but one facet of the play. In this chapter nearly all the examples of figures of speech and meter have been taken from one scene only, Act III, scene iii, had been done with the images in the preceding chapter. This is merely for the sake of convenience. The earnest student will realise what variety and wealth of imagery and rhetoric can be found in the rest of the play. Indeed the rhetorical technique used in the play has been given extraordinary importance by the modern critic Patricia Parker. Making an analysis of several multiplicities of meanings and implications in the play, she says that all these particularise the confusion created by the "double time":

> it might be...also the creation of that rhetorical technique which, like jealousy itself, is capable of suggesting precisely such multiplicity.[37]

References

1. Dorsch, T.S., ed. and transl., *Classical Literary Criticism*, Penguin Books, 1975, p. 83.
2. Bradbrook, M.C., *op.cit.*, p. 45.

3. Fluchère, H., *op.cit.*, p. 152.
4. Quoted by Fluchère, *op.cit.*, p. 159.
5. Dorsch, T.S., *op.cit.*, p. 39.
6. Knight, *op.cit.*, p. 104.
7. Act III, scene iii, ll. 327-29, pp. 112-13.
8. Act III, scene iii, ll. 409-17, p. 118.
9. Act III, scene iii, ll. 460-64, p. 121.
10. Act III, scene iii, ll. 169-71, p. 103.
11. Act III, scene iii, ll. 49-51, p. 96.
12. Act III, scene iii, ll. 389-90, p. 117.
13. Act III, scene iii, ll. 7-9, p. 94.
14. Act III, scene iii, ll. 454-57, pp. 120-21.
15. Act III, scene iii, ll. 91-93, p. 98.
16. Act III, scene iii, ll. 69-72.
17. Act III, scene iii, ll. 102-10, p. 98.
18. Act III, scene iii, l. 121, p. 99.
19. St. John, xxi, 15-7, *The Holy Bible*, New York, American Bible Society, no. date, p. 120.
20. Act III, scene iii, ll. 327-29, pp. 112-13.
21. Act III, scene iii, ll. 361-62, pp. 114-15.
22. Act III, scene iii, ll. 392-93, p. 117.
23. Act III, scene iii, ll. 460-63, p. 121.
24. Fluchère, *op.cit.*, p. 181.
25. Act III, scene iii, ll. 14-17, p. 94.
26. Boas, F.S., ed., *Five Pre-Shakespeare Plays*, O.U.P. , 1934, p. 116.
27. Act III, scene iii, ll. 110-14, p. 98.
28. Act III, scene iii, ll. 19-22, p. 94.
29. Act III, scene iii, l. 32, p. 95.
30. Act III, scene iii, l. 46, p. 95.
31. Act III, scene iii, l. 168, p. 103.
32. Act III, scene iii, l. 335, p. 113.
33. Act III, scene iv, l. 82, p. 128.
34. Act I, scene iii, ll. 202-03, p. 32.
35. Act I, scene iii, ll. 218-19, p. 33.
36. Act IV III, scene iii, ll. 40-43, p. 166.
37. Parker, Patricia, *Shakespeare and Rhetoric in Bloom*, *op.cit.*, p. 119.

12

Critical Reception of *Othello*

Othello has, from the very beginning, been accepted as one of the great tragedies of Shakespeare, Thomas Rymer's being the only denigrating voice. Critics might not have liked the character of Othello, or of Iago, or the importance given to the handkerchief, but few have disagreed with the view that it is one of the greatest tragedies of Shakespeare.

It is now an accepted fact that it is the first of his great tragedies to be written in the Jacobean period. It was performed for the first time on November 1, 1604, at King James's Court. The First Folio was printed in 1623 and a Quarto edition in 1622. The Folio was published by Heminge and Condell and the Quarto by Thomas Walkley. There are some points wherein the two differ from each other.

There have been many adaptations and transformations of Shakespeare's plays. Adaptations are those in which several scenes and speeches have been cut, the language changed and some additions made. Transformations are those in which changes are made both in plot and in characters:

> The typical adaptations include substantial cuts of scenes, speeches...much alteration of language and at least one and usually several important...additions.
>
> In transformations Shakespearean characters move through a partly or wholly non-Shakespearean plot, sometimes with introduction of non-Shakespearean characters.[1]

Transformations thus involve more creative work and many great writers have undertaken the work of transforming Shakespeare's plays:

> This "brightest heaven of inventions" is studded with star of varying brilliance. Shakespearean characters are often simplified or trundled through new events, with the Shakespearean ending scrapped.[2]

Othello also has undergone adaptation and transformation. As productions in England are far too numerous, a few of the famous ones are mentioned below.

In the eighteenth century Jean-Francois Ducis wrote several translated transformations of Shakespeare's plays. He wrote *Hamlet* and *King Lear* with happy endings. As far as *Othello* goes, he went much farther, for he composed the play with two different endings. Victor Hugo had been very much against the handkerchief so Ducis changed it into a diamond bracelet. The play produced by Goethe when he was the theater director at Weimar was an adaptation as it was more or less faithful to Shakespeare. There were many more productions in the nineteenth century. In 1833 the American Negro Ira Aldridge played the role of a black Othello in Covent Garden in London. Another black actor Morgan Smith did the same towards the end of the century and Paul Robeson did the same in 1930. About the same time a Swiss man-of-letters René-Louis Piachaud adapted many plays of Shakespeare, *Othello* among them.

It was roughly at the same time (1937) that George Jean Nathan, an influential American critic of the time, wrote *The Avon Flows*. This was a conglomeration of three different plays of Shakespeare—*Romeo and Juliet*, *Othello* and *The Taming of the Shrew*. It was a play in three Acts. Act I is based on *Romeo and Juliet*. He selects certain passages from Shakespeare and ends the Act with Friar Lawrence uniting Romeo and Juliet in marriage. In Act II these star-crossed lovers become Othello and Desdemona though they keep the same names as in Act I, and Tybalt becomes Iago. This Act ends where the fourth Act of *Othello* does, with a jealous Romeo striking Desdemona and kicking Tybalt. Desdemona's words on fidelity are given to

Romeo. In Act III Romeo triumphs, like Petrucchio, by dominating Juliet. The play thus has a happy ending. The work is more or less a burlesque, yet it is important in that it foreshadows the technique of collage which later became the rage.

Literary criticism, except for Rymer in the seventeenth century and, in a limited manner, T.S. Eliot and F.R. Leavis in the twentieth, has been favourable. Rymer's condemnation of the play is a wholesale affair, for he disapproved of every feature of the play and ended:

> The tragic part is plainly none other than a Bloody farce, without salt or savour.[3]

The most important critic of the next century, Dr. Johnson, took a far more balanced view. As always, his is the attitude of a serious and responsible critic. He approves of every aspect of the play:

> The beauties of this play impress themselves so strongly upon the attention of the reader, that they can draw no aid from critical illustration.[4]

With his usual acuteness of perception Dr. Johnson had pointed out that the plot, if the first Act is omitted, is that of a most successfully constructed classical play, and later critics have built upon this:

> Had the scene opened in Cyprus and the preceding incidents been occasionally related, there had been little wanting to a drama of the most exact and scrupulous regularity.[5]

Criticism underwent a most important change in its very basics in the nineteenth century with the exploration of the depths of the human psyche and also on the depiction of emotions. Thus Hazlitt has observed very acutely:

> It has been observed that Shakespeare's characters are constructed upon deep psychological principles; and there is something in this play which is very like it.[6]

In the twentieth century also, the approach of Coleridge, the greatest critic among the Romantics, has been deferred to. His comment on Iago has been handed down with reverence:

> The last speech, [Iago soliloquy], the motive-hunting of motiveless malignity—how awful! In itself fiendish; while yet he was allowed to bear the divine image, too fiendish for his own steady view.[7]

In the last century literary critics started to analyse different aspects of the play, like the theme, the plot, the art of characterisation, etc. These features had been commented upon earlier also, but detailed studies had not been made. Revival of interest in many Elizabethan elements like its psychology, philosophy and cosmology has led to analyses of the plays from these points of view as well. The works of Lily B. Campbell, Theodore Spencer and others have been of great value in this respect.

The sources from which the poet had taken the material for his plays have always intrigued literary critics and G. Bullough has made a thorough study of these. His work in this field is not only a pioneering work but an authoritative one also (*vide* Chapter 9 *supra*).

The imagery of Shakespeare's plays has been studied by Caroline Spurgeon and W. Clemen and their contribution to Shakespearean studies have been invaluable. Their opinions have been considered in the relevant context (*vide* Chapter 10, *supra*).

Late twentieth century brought forth many critical essays following the methods of the many new schools of criticism that have sprung up recently—like structuralism, formalism, etc. The views of the critics of the Feminist school as well as those of others have been referred to in the relevant context. Indian schools of criticism have also seen a revival of interest, though not much work has been done in this field. One such attempt shall now be given, studying the play from the viewpoint of the Rasavāda.

Indian Dramaturgy

According to Indian dramatic theory, there are ten kinds of *rūpakas*. *Ācārya* Dhananjaya's work, the *Daśarūpaka* is accepted as one of the definitive works in this field. He has pointed out that this classification has been done in accordance with three factors: the content, the character and *aṅgī-rasa*.

Vastu, netā, rasāṣṭesān bhedako vastu ca tridhā.[8]

The subject-matter, the hero and the rasas, these are the three that give rise to the differences among plays.

According to this division *Othello* will be a *nāṭaka*. Dhananjaya tells us that the hero of such a play should be *dhīrodātta* by nature, of high lineage and that if in the story there are incidents that go against the hero's nature or the rasa of the play then these should be either modified or omitted.[9] When Shakespeare adapted Cinthio's story, he transfigured it so that Othello gained tragic dignity (*vide* Sources of *Othello* in Chapter 9, *supra*).

The *aṅgī-rasa* of a *nāṭaka* should be either the *vīra* or *śṛṅgāra rasa*. There is scope for debate in this matter as far as *Othello* is concerned. Now, *Othello* is a tragedy and Sanskrit dramatic theory does not have a sympathetic attitude towards tragedies. Tragedy generate *karuna* rasa. It is the capacity of the poet to help the reader establish identification or tādātmya with the hero that leads to universalisation (*sādhāraṇīkaraṇa*). In the case of *karuṇa* rasa, this is eminently possible and, as such, tragedy could have been taken as a successful form of drama. Yet, since *karuṇa* rasa makes identification possible, tragedies can be easily studied from the viewpoint of *rasavāda*.

For the purposes of the present argument, it can be said that though *karuṇa* dominates at the end, it is not the *aṅgī* of the play. The *aṅgī-rasa* is *śṛṅgāra*. There are three conditions for the *aṅgī*: (a) *vahuvyapti*—that it should be present throughout the play (b) that the main characters should be motivated by it (c) *phalāgama*—that the main objective of the play should support it. All these three conditions are fulfilled in our play. Taking the first condition first, throughout the play love is the one emotion that dominates over all the others. All the characters except Iago are impelled by love in one form or another, specially Othello and Desdemona. Roderigo loves Desdemona and follows the married couple to Cyprus. It is Othello's love for Desdemona that brings about the tragic end of the play. A detailed analysis of the play, which will not be undertaken here, will show how, from the beginning to the end, *śṛṅgāra* dominates the scenes.

At the end *karuna* triumphs, but it should be remembered that *śṛṅgāra* has led to its generation.

There is no question that all the main characters except for Iago are motivated by love. Iago is the *prati-nāyaka* (villain) and can be excepted. Cassio's dalliance with Bianca leads to the fight at the end. Roderigo's love for Desdemona leads to his tragic end. Bianca's love for Cassio is genuine and enduring. As far as Othello and Desdemona are concerned, it is their love for each other that is the motive power of the play. Not only does *śṛṅgāra* permeate the play, it motivates the characters as well.

It is when the factor of *phalāgama* is concerned that doubt arises. As has been pointed out above, in tragedy the *phalāgama* is negative event. The desired *phalāgama* of a play with love dominating it is marriage, which is not the case here. It is *karuṇa* rasa that dominates in the last scene. It has also been pointed out above that this fact does not invalidate the claims of *śṛṅgāra* as the *aṅgī-rasa* of the play.

The plot of any play is divisible into two main sections. The main plot is known as *adhikārika* and the related story as *prāsaṅgika*. This latter, in its turn, is divided into two kinds, *patākā* and *prakarī*. In our play, the Othello-Desdemona-Iago plot is the *adhikārika*. *Patākās* continue till the end of the play and the events connected with Roderigo can be called such. The incidents connected with Cassio and Bianca, the drinking-scenes, the scenes in the first Act are all *prakarīs*. They last for a short time only, though the progress of the plot is influenced by them. *Prakarīs* do not continue till the end.

Indian dramaturgy has divided the progress of the plot into several stages. It is a complex division and each division has different characteristics. There are five basic parts:

Bīja-bindu-patākākhya-prakarī-kārya lakṣaṇa[10]

Bīja (seed), *bindu* (point), *patākā*, *prakarī* and *kārya* (deeds)—and there are more stages in a play in between these five. If the plot of *Othello* is analysed stage by stage then it will be seen how each one of them can be found in it, only here the *niyatāpti* and *phalāgama* are negative ones.

As far as the characters are concerned, Othello has many characteristics of the *dhīrodātta* hero. Dhananjaya tells us that such a hero is a steady man, grave in demeanour and forgiving by nature. He never indulges in self-praise but he has a quiet pride and great resolution in him[11]:

> Mahāsattvo-atigambhīrah kshamāvānavikatthanah
> Sthiro nigurḥāṇkāro dhīrodatto dṛhavratah.[12]

This comes very near to Aristotle's the Great Souled Man, which is one of the most important characters given by him in his *Ethics*. Othello fails to fulfil two of the requirements of such a hero. He is not a *mahasttva* or a steady man who remains unruffled by joys and sorrows. He is calm and steady in the battlefield—there are repeated references to this by the other characters. Lodovico describes him as a man "whom passion could not shake". But we know that Othello's nature is not unimpregnable. He himself tells us that he is:

> One not easily jealous, but being wrought,
> Perplex'd in the extreme.[13]

We also know that he is not forgiving by nature as he penalises Cassio by dismissing him and later cannot bring himself to forgive either him or Desdemona. In these two particulars, he falls short of a *dhīrodātta* hero. The others he fulfills.

As far as Desdemona is concerned, Shakespeare's heroines, as it is, defy categorisation. These are many kinds of heroines in Sanskrit poetics. The one that Desdemona approaches the nearest is the *madhyā-dhīrā nāyikā*. Such a heroine chides her beloved with smiles and irony, as indeed Desdemona does in Act III, scene iii when she pleads for Cassio before the temptation begins. In other respects, she is an ideal heroine as she has most of the twenty womanly graces (*alaṇkāra*) that a heroine is supposed to have. Of *bhāva, hāva, helā, śobhā, kānti, dīpti, mādhurya, pragalbhatā, aüdārya* and *dhairya*, the first ten of the graces she possesses all, as a careful reading can show. She also has many of the next ten.

An analysis of Othello's famous soliloquy "it is the cause" from the *rasa* point of view will be given now to show the relevance of this method when applied to Shakespeare. Where a western critic would find dramatic irony, effective images, etc. in it, this method will show that it ascends to the high level in which the experience it affords is called *brahamasvāda-sahodrā*. Othello, torn by the conflict of anger, jealousy, love and pity, becomes the *āśraya* of all these powerful emotions. The attendant *vyabhicārī* emotions of *nirveda* (despair), *glani* (weariness), *amarṣa* (vengefulness) are there as well as the *vibhāva* of admiration of Desdemona's beauty:

> Thou cunning'st pattern of excelling nature
> ... ...
> Ah, balmy breath, that doth almost persuade
> Justice to break her sword.[14]

Othello's pity, accompanied by the *anubhāva* of tears, is recognized by him to be heavenly:

> I must weep
> But they are cruel tears; this sorrow's heavenly.[15]

In other words he has, in the intensity of his emotions, ascended to a level beyond the mortal one. In this one speech of twenty-two lines, Shakespeare takes the very essence of jealousy, love, anger, terror and pity and distils a unique mixture *śṛṅgāra* and *karuṇa* with undertones of *raudra* and *bhayānaka*. Othello is the universal, archetypal figure of the betrayed husband and with him as the *āśraya* the reader or the spectator experiences all the different rasas mentioned just now. This of course, is very cursory account of the speech.

Indeed the above discussion is extremely sketchy and brief. It merely affords a glimpse into the riches that can be revealed if a more detailed study of the play is undertaken from the point of view of any of the schools of Indian poetics: *rasa, dhvani, alaṅkāra* or anything else. A slightly more detailed anaylsis from the *rasa-vāda* point of view, however, had been done earlier.

References

1. Cohn, Ruby, *Modern Shakespearean Offshoots*, New Jersey, Princeton University Press, 1976, pp. 3-4.
2. *Ibid.*, p. 4.
3. Wain, *op.cit.*, p. 49.
4. *Ibid.*, p. 50.
5. *Ibid.*, p. 51.
6. Price, A., *op.cit.*, p. 31.
7. Wain, *op.cit.*
8. Dwivedi, Hazari Prasad and Dwivedi, Prithvinath, *Nāṭya-Śastra ki Paramparā our Daśarūpaka*, New Delhi, Rajkamal Prakashan, 1971, p. 67.
9. Haas, George C.O. Translated, *The Daśarupa: A Treatise on Hindu Dramaturgy*, Delhi, Motilal Banarsidass, 1962, p. 33.
10. Dwivedi, *op.cit.*, p. 71.
11. Haas, *op.cit.*, p. 41.
12. Act IV, scene ii, ll. 346-47, p. 195.
13. Act V, scene ii, ll. 11, 16-17, p. 178.
14. Act V, scene ii, ll. 20-21, pp. 178-79.
15. "Shakespeare in the Light of Sanskrit Poetics", *Mother India*, March 1993-July 1993 by the present writer.

Some Important Questions

1. Consider *Othello* as a tragedy of misunderstanding.
2. "*Othello* is eminently a domestic tragedy." Do you agree? Give reasons for your answer.
3. "The play turns on this theme: the cynical intellect pitted against a loving humanity." Elucidate.
4. "Love and sex are the opposite of the play, not coming together." Comment, with special reference to *Othello*.
5. "Othello becomes automatically a symbol of faith in human values of love, of war, of romance." Analyse the character of Othello in the light of this remark.
6. Do you agree with the view that Desdemona "becomes a symbol of man's ideal, the supreme value of love"?
7. "Iago is utterly devilish: there is no weakness in his casing armour of unrepentant villainy." Elucidate.
8. The poetry of *Othello* has been described as "the noble *Othello* music". Write an essay on the style of *Othello* in the light of this remark.
9. *Othello* comes much nearer than any of Shakespeare's great plays to observe the unities." Expound the plot of *Othello* in the light [illegible] .iis remark.
10. Write an essay on the double time-scheme in *Othello*.
11. Write a note on the imagery of *Othello*.
12. Write a note on the theme of love and revenge in *Othello*.

Select Bibliography

Bayley, John, *Shakespeare and Tragedy*, London, Routledge and Kegan Paul, 1981.

Bradbrook, M.C., *Themes and Conventions of Elizabethan Tragedy*, Cambridge University Press, 1935.

——, *Elizabethan Stage Conditions*, Cambridge, 1968.

Bradley, A.C., *Shakespearean Tragedy*, London, Macmillan, 1960.

Bratchell, D.F., ed., *Shakespearean Tragedy*, London, Routledge, 1990.

Bloom, Harold, ed., *Modern Critical Interpretations Series on Othello*, Delhi, Worldview Pubs., 1987.

Campbell, Lily B., *Shakespeare's Tragic Heroes*, Cambr. Univ. Press, 1930.

Clemen, W., *The Development of Shakespeare's Imagery*, London, Methuen, 1951.

Evans, B., *Shakespeare's Tragic Practice*, Oxford, 1978.

Knight, G. Wilson, *The Wheel of Fire,* Oxford University Press, 1938.

Leech, Clifford, *Shakespeare's Tragedies*, London, Chatto & Windus, 1950.

Ridley, M.R., *Othello*, Arden Shakespeare, London, Methuen, 1984.

Spencer, Theodore, *Shakespeare and the Nature of Man*, New York, Macmillan, 1945.

Wain, John, ed., *Othello: A Casebook*, New York, Palgrave, 1994.

Index